GIFTS OF
Gratitude

*A Journey of Remembrance
and Connection*

by
Jennifer Burchill

Published by hope*books
2217 Matthews Township Pkwy
Suite D302
Matthews, NC 28105
www.hopebooks.com

hope*books is a division of hope*media

Printed in the United States of America

First paperback edition.

Paperback ISBN: 979-8-89185-138-2
Hardcover ISBN: 979-8-89185-139-9
Ebook ISBN: 979-8-89185-140-5
Library of Congress Number: 2024948861

Scripture quotations are taken from the Holy Bible, New Living Translation, copyright ©1996, 2004, 2015 by Tyndale House Foundation. Used by permission of Tyndale House Publishers, Carol Stream, Illinois 60188. All rights reserved.

hope✳books
hopebooks.com
*Because the world needs your hope-filled
words now more than ever.*

~ For Max and Charlotte, the greatest gifts I've ever received ~

CONTENTS

CHAPTER 1

REFLECTING ON WHAT MATTERS

"Of all the words of mice and men, the saddest are,
'It might have been." —*Kurt Vonnegut*[1]

If you do not have your own pandemic story, you have no doubt heard one from someone you know, as this time affected us all in some way—the jumbled emotions, feeling isolated, worrying about family and friends, and the never-ending unknown. We found ourselves in a situation we could not have envisioned, an untethering. We were glued to the news as a necessity to learn as the experts were learning: what new discovery or hunch has been uncovered today? What are the latest numbers? Will this ever get better? We had to discover new ways to show love and support and to feel connection as we were unable to physically be in the presence of others. The stories laden with grief were everywhere. Each day brought a new tale of sadness, of so many loved ones dying and their family and friends not being able to be with them to say goodbye. I learned about a college

---

[1] Vonnegut, Kurt. *Slaughterhouse-Five*. Delacorte Press, 1969. The quote is in reference to Steinbeck, John. *Of Mice and Men*. Viking Press, 1937.

friend who went into the hospital and never came home; her parents unable to visit, to hold her hand, to comfort her, to say goodbye. It was heartbreaking on a collective human level.

I'm writing this (thankfully) post-pandemic. The Covid outbreak seems mostly managed, but still, world affairs remain in such a state that it's easy to understand why there is a pervasive sense of despair blanketing the world. Social media, for all its ability to "connect" us, is a frenzy of comparison and consumerism that is affecting our children and likely the emotional well-being of us all.

And yet—amidst that, I am struck by the moments of kindness I see sprinkled throughout my day: a smile shared with the mother in the checkout line at Target when she knew I overheard her toddler's remark about something that only a child would notice...a flash of connection. It's the friendly wave and nod by the older gentleman with the flappy-eared hat and khaki jacket that walks by every morning with his Scottie dog who sports his own tiny plaid dog jacket. These little moments shared make us feel seen, reminding us of our sense of the human experience. It's a warmth we feel on an internal, innate level, as we are beings who are wired for connection to our very core.

And I can't help but reflect on how these little moments that are woven throughout our days intertwine with the bigger moments: the championing inspiration, the quiet support, the probing conversations, the moments of shared joy. They string together to form a lifetime of connectedness, and when we actually take the time to reflect on them, we realize we're grateful.

~

Gratitude is just plain good for us– emotionally and physically. There have been several studies that show the physiological and neurological benefits: that gratitude helps with stress, resiliency, even grief. In Cornelius Platinga Jr.'s book, *Gratitude*, a whole chapter is devoted to the many benefits and the studies behind them.[2] Feeling grateful for what we have in the present moment and reminiscing about our happy memories changes our brain chemicals, releasing the neurotransmitters dopamine and serotonin thus altering our mood toward the positive.[3] Sharing that gratitude allows the wave to continue its momentum and reach the recipient too.

However, we're collectively missing out on not only taking the time to reflect and fully allowing the joy of that moment to wash over us but also in the "passing it on"—and seizing the opportunity to share the gift of these moments with those who contributed to or were there to experience them with us. Often, we don't convey or even realize what someone meant to us or the effect they had on our lives until they're no longer there. Then, in addition to the grief of saying goodbye there's the sting of regret—for the sense of not being able to

---

[2] Plantinga, Cornelius, Jr. *Gratitude*. Brazos Press, 2024. Chapter 4, "What Happens to Me If I Am Grateful."

[3] PositivePsychology.com. "The Neuroscience of Gratitude and How It Affects Anxiety & Grief." *Positive Psychology*, 28 Aug. 2021, https://positivepsychology.com/neuroscience-of-gratitude/#brain-effects. Accessed 19 Aug. 2024.

thank someone for what they taught us, how they loved us. And we miss out on telling others how they matter, enhancing their story, enhancing our own, contributing to their legacy and to ours.

How much more gratifying would it be to share with those who we love how thankful we are for the role they have played in our lives **while they are here to hear these sentiments**- to share these gifts of gratitude?

That is the purpose of this book—to serve as a guide in helping you recall the people you've encountered who gave you these moments, these lessons, these kindnesses, and then to encourage ways for you to share them back with them.

People matter; don't wait.

⁓

I was extremely close with both of my grandmothers and one of my grandfathers.

My Poppa had Alzheimer's disease when it was still a new diagnosis and wasn't well understood in the mid-80s. It was thought to be the result of a head injury, a silly, split-second accident where he hit his head and was knocked unconscious while painting a house. He later also developed Parkinson's, and he was slowly declining cognitively and physically.

My grandparents lived about four hours away, and I remember during one of my visits from college, he had an uncharacteristic moment of frustration with an angry outburst. This was not at all what I had ever experienced of my Poppa, watching him as he stormed out of the room as fast as he was able to, clunking his walker along, with purpose, to the back bedroom.

I went into the den where my grandmother was and just lost it, sobbing to her, and I knew she understood how I was feeling. I got the sense from her that this was not uncommon, that she had seen similar behavior and was used to navigating the sudden ups and downs.

While she comforted me, enveloping me in a big hug, Poppa came into the room as if nothing had happened. He was back to his normal, sweet demeanor. He asked if I was crying because of him. I nodded, which made me sob even harder, choking to just try and get it out. In his moment of lucidness, he said something that offered a profound explanation—one that helped me make sense of his condition and changed the way I looked at him and the situation. He told me not to cry for him because he wasn't aware of what was happening when he lost his temper, acted differently, or couldn't remember something; he wasn't in any pain, there was no frustration or sadness for him, it just was what it was in that moment and then the moment was gone. He said he knew it was harder for me and others, but especially for my Grandmommy because we had to watch him act in a way that wasn't like the person we knew. Through his insight, I felt a sense of relief that he understood how it was affecting us. I was touched that he could empathize with us when we were trying to empathize with him.

Because of his slow decline, I had some time to process his condition as best as a college kid can. Although I did not completely understand why his personality was often different each time I saw him, nor how he could confuse me with his mother ("Have you finished whitewashing the fence?"), I was able to make more trips to see him on school breaks. I had the chance to let him know how much he meant to me. I wrote him letters and left little love notes and drawings, lots of XOXOs on the chalkboard. I told him how I loved the sound of his giggle, how he taught me to appreciate big band music and inspired my love of movies. I shared how I remembered that he was the one who took me to see my first professional musical, Annie, at The Shubert Theater in Chicago for my 10th birthday. I recognized how he modeled family loyalty and honoring promises made by taking care of my great-grandmother for the remainder of her life after her husband died.

His death was devastating to me in my early 20s because it was the first loss I experienced of someone I was close to. But even then, I felt a sense of completeness—I did not feel like anything went unsaid. I was able to linger in the moments with him a little longer—to hold an embrace an extra few seconds, to soak in the smell of his aftershave. I knew that he knew what a difference he made in my life, the impact he had, and there were no regrets. I felt our conversations after he got sick brought us closer and certainly gave me an enhanced view and appreciation of him. I knew he loved me, and he knew how deeply I loved him. Thinking of that giggle of his always makes me smile.

It was a different story, however, with my grandmothers. Both of them passed without my having the chance to say goodbye, to tell them the depth of my love and the particular reasons why I loved them. I did not have the chance to thank them for all of the amazing opportunities I had because of them, and it has left me with a deep sense of longing, sadness, and regret.

My "Grandmommy" died when I was overseas on a trip during Christmas. She went into the hospital for a routine procedure but complications arose. She died in the hospital. I found out about this news while at the airport overseas, waiting for our canceled flight to be rescheduled.

I did not have the chance to tell her how thankful I was for the love of reading that I suspect I got from her and how I appreciated how she shared great books with me. On the inside cover of her books she inscribed, "Please read, enjoy and return to Harriet." (I thought that was so classy.) I loved how she always had her "face on" and that everything about visiting her felt special: proper table settings, even for takeout. Fong's Chinese food was removed from the paper containers and artfully displayed on the fancy dishes. A scoop of ice cream was set out in her best bowls, with cloth napkins. She was a good listener, and I often confided in her. She was an avid and reliable pen pal; I always recognized her handwriting and her black felt tip pen when the envelopes arrived. I loved going with her to her bridge group. She showed me off and presented me to her friends as if I were the guest of honor, and I was allowed to sit and peruse the coffee table books and enjoy dessert on china plates along with the ladies. I felt like we were two peas in a pod, both Virgos, a fact she reminded me of often, "Did you see our horoscope today?"

One thing I am thankful for was that I shared the news of my pregnancy with her before I left on that trip. We weren't telling anyone yet because it was early in the first trimester, but my mom thought it would be a boost for her to be in on the secret, so I called and let her know before I left. She was, in her words, "tickled" and said she had a feeling I was going to have a boy (which I did) and that I should name him Spencer because she always regretted not naming my uncle Spencer (which I did not.) It was near the top of the list, though.

I also did not have a chance to say goodbye to my other grandmother, who we all called GrandmaGay, as if it were one word. She suffered a stroke on a Sunday evening in early February and never again regained consciousness. I had visited her at Christmas, which ended up being the last time I saw her. We have a 4-generation photo (of her, my dad, me, and my 4-month-old son) from that visit, which is one of my most cherished photos. I was so thankful she was able to meet my son. She had been a nurse, and when we were there and he started crying, she instinctively reached out her arms from her wheelchair and said, "Here, give him to me." And when I did, he quieted immediately. A nurse and a mother to three boys herself, she sure knew what she was doing. Interestingly, when she found out I was pregnant, she also predicted a boy and said, "You're going to have a boy, and he's going to be over nine pounds like mine all were." She was spot on—he weighed in at 9 lbs, 3 oz.

I've been told I help keep Hallmark in business with all of the cards I send, and GrandmaGay said that no matter what, she could count on the fact that she would receive at least one card for every holiday from her Jennifer. That remark still makes me smile, and I think about it every time I mail out my Valentine's, St. Patrick's Day, Easter, Thanksgiving, and Christmas cards. I am thankful for how supportive she was of whatever activity I was participating in at the time and how she made sure I had the opportunity to experience new things, like seeing the World's Fair and traveling to Europe. She modeled hard work and self-sufficiency, and through her often repeated saying, she reminded me to always "count my blessings."

~

I feel a sense of urgency around remembering and expressing thankfulness these days, and it is heightened by the fact that my dad is now in declining health himself, diagnosed with a terminal illness. I want to be able to share gratitude with him and my mom for everything they've given me, taught me, shared with me, and how they've loved me. There is something that reaching a certain decade does to you—it encourages looking back and reflecting on pivotal moments and uncovering some of the poignant yet more subtle ones. I am at that age where every week I see another post from a friend who has lost a parent, a friend, a mentor. Some have shared how they wish they had said something, reached out, and shared more before it was too late. Why do we wait until we're writing someone's eulogy to realize what they meant to us? We regret leaving things unsaid, overcome with that sense of *I wish I'd told them...* And this is the heart of it: we often don't say what we think or feel or appreciate, thinking we have all the time in the world, and then sadly, it's too late, and we are left with what could have been said or shared.

But we can remedy this. Since my dad's diagnosis, I have started to be more aware of these moments in my own life and have been sharing these "thank you notes." Doing this has had a ripple effect by conjuring up even more memories. When I share them with others, what I hear most often is, "I never knew..." or "I didn't remember that."

I feel drawn to help others avoid feeling the same sense of regret. I have witnessed firsthand what a difference it makes to be able to express that thanks and then, on the flip side, how receiving that thanks impacts them. I've seen what a difference it makes to hear words of thanks, to watch people soulfully connect. My dad was a professor, athletic director, and coach of multiple sports for over 30 years. Always a private and humble man, when he was diagnosed with a terminal illness and first began declining in health, he did not want his illness shared. However, being from a small town, word tends to spread, and he has been contacted by many.

We have been moved and, frankly, humbled by the outpouring of support, love, and gratitude expressed to him. Former assistant coaches and players have traveled hours to visit him to reminisce and to express their thanks. There was one story, in particular, of a player from the 80s who said he wouldn't have graduated if it weren't for my dad, reminding him that he had let him practice when he was on academic probation. This player said that it made a difference for him, being able to still feel and be treated like part of the team. He's received letters, and one was written to the facility where he lives, letting them know what a legend they are caring for. Wow, how our family will always cherish that. And we've heard his former players tell him that they love him. I choke up when I think about it, but I am so, so thankful they were able to share this with him and that he was able to hear this gratitude. It has made a difference not only to him but also to our family. It allows his grandchildren to know the kind of man he was before he was old and sick, the impact he had, and how much he was loved. (Thank you, Troy, Darren, Steve, Al, Tim, and Darryl- you touched us with your kindness.)

We all have different experiences, moments, and memories we're thankful for—and for the people we shared them with. I am sharing some of mine here in this book. There is much in my more recent years I am grateful for, but I wanted to mostly focus on the growing up years, the 1970s and 80s, for a couple of reasons. First, because as my memory fades, I want to remember and record these times while I still can. Even though the details are a little fuzzy, clouded by a childhood understanding and hazy half-memories, reflecting on them helps me recall some of the details, songs, smells, feelings. And second, because the childhood years shape who we become. I wanted to capture some of the people and experiences who shaped me during this time. These experiences occurred during my formative years, before the responsibilities of being an adult, a mom, and working dimmed the light of awe and wonder a bit. I wanted to uncover it, brush the dust off, hold it up and look, relish, and be thankful, immerse myself in gratitude.

I am capturing these as best and as truthfully as I can remember, but my disclaimer is that my truth might not be THE truth of these stories or the truth of anyone referenced in these stories. I hope I do them justice and that you are left with the message of gratitude and appreciation and that you can forgive any discrepancies.

Each chapter tells a few personal stories intended to stir up and elicit memories of your own. Each concludes with some prompts for action. Revel in the moments and reflect what they have meant to you. I encourage you to reach out and have conversations with those who have impacted your lives in a positive and meaningful way. Let them know what it meant to you, through a message or letter, a retelling of the story with others, or simply a prayer of thanks for the gift of that moment. Allow these moments of appreciation and connection to provide you with a sense of peace and of closure. Experience the completeness of having shared, so there is no question of just how deeply they matter to us and so you don't have to say, "I wish they'd known." And through this, we can contribute to their legacy and to ours, a legacy of love.

GETTING STARTED

Instead of waiting until whenever, I invite you to act upon this right away, like now. It might feel overwhelming to reflect on past moments of wonder, awe, and hope amidst the hustle and bustle of life, the grief over the news we see and hear, and the comparison of ourselves to others. It takes some focus to reflect, and it is a muscle to exercise. It requires a deep breath, quiet thought, and contemplation. But when you get started, it's like a ball of string. You unravel more and more, and surprising things resurface.

Some of the more practical ways to feel this joy and connection are to go through old photos or mementos, listen to songs, reflect on a time that someone made you feel important, confident, loved, supported, listened to, able to conquer the world, etc. Then, reach out and thank them. It doesn't have to be an awkward or formal conversation or particularly eloquent; just let it be from the heart and what feels natural to you. Something as simple as, "Hey, remember when..." or "I just wanted to say..." Chances are they don't even know how much it meant to you, and who knows, you may even change their outlook for the day.

Connect with them to show them your appreciation, whether it be:

- Tagging them in a social media post to share your gratitude (a friend reached out to me recently in this way and it made my day!)
- Sending an email recalling what they did and why it meant so much to you
- Sharing an old photo that captures the time you want to share
- Sharing a song that reminds you of an adventure
- Calling them for a good long chat
- Sharing a big old hug when you see them next
- Or my favorite—mailing a handwritten letter, because even in this day and age of instant, abbreviated, emoji-filled messages, everyone still loves going to the mailbox and seeing a handwritten treasure amongst catalogs or junk mail.

And for those who are no longer with us, share these remembrances with their family or friends and contribute to their legacy. Help them understand how their loved one touched the lives of others. It can be satisfying to the soul to remember them—their unique qualities, the essence of what made them special, and to recall stories that we can pass on to future generations. In reminiscing with others about them, we may possibly even discover something new.

If you cannot reach anyone, you can always say a little prayer of thanks for their impact, for crossing your path when they did, or send gratitude into the Universe.

There aren't many guarantees in life, but one we all share is that our time on Earth is finite. And at the end of our time here, we want to feel as though we mattered, that we made a difference, used our God-given talents the best we could, and that we left this planet a little better than we found it—even if in some small way.

> "They may forget what you said — but they will
> never forget how you made them feel."
> —Carl W. Buehner."[4]

Let's share the appreciation, the gratitude. Let them know how they made us feel. My wish is that this sparks reflection and inspires you to connect to those cherished memories and people and show them that they matter and the impact they have had. I hope that you experience an enhanced gratitude and sense of completeness in being able to share. May this initiate many happy memories and reasons for gratitude.

---

[4] Evans, Richard L. *Richard Evans' Quote Book*. Publishers Press, 1971.

CHAPTER 2

GRATEFUL FOR THE KINDNESS OF STRANGERS

D o you remember your first airplane ride? Likely, you were with a family member who helped you navigate the experience: what to have ready to show the gate agent, how to place your items overhead or stuff them under your seat, how to buckle in. Mine was by myself, a 15-year-old from a small farm town in middle America, whose stomach butterflies were a combination of not knowing what to expect coupled with excitement. That first plane ride (where I learned how essential it is to pop your ears when flying) wasn't a quick trip to Chicago or New York, but to a foreign country—where I didn't speak the language, and it wasn't just for a couple weeks, but for an entire year. Can you imagine going to live with host families for months at a time that you have never met? And this was at a time when text messages did not exist, nor household email. When international telephone calls were so prohibitively expensive that on the rare occasion you could make one, they were truly a splurge, and you had to talk really, really fast to try to keep it under three minutes. Well, that was me the summer before my junior year of high school. I flew from Miami to Rio de Janeiro before my final destination of Vitoria, Brazil, to begin a year-long exchange program.

STRANGERS WHO BECAME FAMILY

When I arrived at the airport that day in August, I walked down the stairs from the small airplane and was greeted on the tarmac by a homemade sign with my name (spelled with one N and two Fs) and several unfamiliar faces, all eager to introduce themselves. Members from two of the three families I would be living with were there, along with some curious friends. I was tired, feeling unsure, and definitely like a novelty on display, but also eager to settle in. I remember the ride to my first host family's house, finding it jarring to hear Dire Straits' "Money for Nothing" on the radio and then the DJ speaking Portuguese. I often felt surprised during those first few months at hearing something familiar but in a foreign language. I paused and had to look each time I heard He-Man on the TV exclaim, "I have the power" with such feeling—but in Portuguese, "Eu tenho a forca!" It made him sound less powerful to me.

My first family had three children, a son and daughter older than me and then a son the same age as my youngest brother. Upon arriving, we had a snack, and they asked if I knew any Portuguese. I proudly belted out the only phrase I knew, one that I had learned as a "must-know" on the plane from another foreign exchange student and practiced: "Where is the bathroom?" This prompted my new mother to hop up and quickly escort me by the elbow to the bathroom. I was confused by this misunderstanding, and it took a few attempts before she and the others understood that I actually didn't need to go. I was just showing off what I knew.

I learned that my first host sister, Patricia, although only a year older than me, was not a student at the same school that I would be attending. She was at university, and I would be attending a primary and secondary school, Sacred Heart of Mary, where I'd need to wear a uniform(!) Outside of school, though, Patricia quickly became my keeper, whether that was a role she wanted or not. She gave up her bedroom and moved into her grandmother's suite so that I could have my own space in their beautiful stucco home, with stained glass windows and deeply hued tiles. It was so different from the sculpted green scratchy carpet I was used to walking on every day. Those first few weeks I was in disbelief and awe of my new surroundings amidst palm and mango trees— and wow, to have a pool!

Patricia not only shared her room, she shared her friends, allowing me to tag along when they went out on weekend nights, giving me the experience of being a teenager in the 80s in a beachside town. She introduced me to so many things: popular music groups, Brazilian bikinis, pão de queijo (cheese bread that is so melt-in-your-mouth delicious that it's hard to stop eating), and local Brazilian chocolates, made with cocoa beans supplied by my host father, and even (shhh, don't tell my host mom) John Player Special cigarettes!

Even better than introducing me to new things, Patricia always made sure I was included. Before I was fluent enough to carry on an intelligible conversation, which took about 3-4 months, I often struggled, feeling detached in social situations. I would concentrate so hard to catch words and phrases and try to piece things together and keep up, but I was quickly left behind and would end up spacing out. Patricia was the one who would notice; she could see it in my eyes (deer-in-the-headlights phenomenon perhaps?), and she would bring me back in and make sure that I could understand. In the beginning, this meant that she would translate into English for me. However, after a couple weeks of being there, just when I started feeling like I was settling in and comfortable, I came bounding down the stairs one morning to dig into the freshly baked baguettes as the other family members did. But there was a surprise for me at the breakfast table, when I asked a question and my mother simply responded, "no mas Ingles." I looked at my father, and he confirmed and repeated, "No mas Ingles." After the panic wore off, understanding that they would be speaking "no more English," I figured that meant that I was going to be pretty quiet for a while.

My family immersed me so that I could learn and have the full experience—I didn't come that far just to speak English. And from that moment on, Patricia found a way to explain to me in Portuguese whenever I did not understand by repeating it slowly and clearly enunciating, often including animated hand gestures (nice ones, of course). When we'd get stuck, she would point to a word in my ever-present little yellow pocket dictionary. And before I moved in with my second family that January, I was able to hold a conversation. I felt much more comfortable and maybe even a little smug at how much better my Portuguese was compared to a couple of other American exchange students I had met.

I appreciate the exchange year experience on another level now, having raised children of my own. I'm humbled and astounded that there were three families who would welcome me into their homes and agree to take care of a stranger like their own child. But they did, and we have continued to stay in touch over the years. One year, Patricia even came to visit me in my town to experience attending a January term class at the college where my father taught. I was thrilled she was able to meet the friends I had talked about while in Brazil and spend the holidays with my family, including a trip to meet both sides of the extended family up in the Chicago area. Exchanging sunshine and a pool for Midwest gray skies and snow must have been a shock for her, but she was a good sport, going everywhere we dragged her.

And then, years later, for my 40th birthday, I returned to Brazil for the first time since I'd left that July afternoon. This time, I was welcomed into Patricia's home she shares with her husband and son. Although it had been 25 years since I had been there, it was as if no time had passed between us; we quickly fell back into our routine, our dynamic. Although now adults, the mannerisms, speech patterns, and the dance of how we communicated were exactly the same. If I didn't understand something someone said, I'd immediately look at her, and she instinctively slowed down and repeated for me, still looking out for me all those years later, falling right back into her role of big sister. We change, yet we stay the same.

After years of exchanging Christmas cards, which later became emails and, more recently, Instagram messages, I was devastated to learn (through an Instagram post, actually) that the only big sister I ever had, my dear, sweet Patricia, recently lost her battle with a lengthy illness. My heart sank in disbelief, and I reached out to other friends and family to confirm I was translating correctly what I was reading. I didn't know she had been sick, and in addition to the waves of shock and sadness, there was a crumpling of regret. A regret that I never explicitly expressed to her how deeply thankful I am for her—for everything she did for me and for her place in my story.

If I could write her a thank you letter or have one last conversation, this is what I'd tell her:

Querida (Dear) Patricia,

Thank you for looking out for me like only a big sister can, giving me your bedroom, and letting me tag along when you went out with Catia and Claudia. Thank you for stepping out of a conversation to bring me into it. Thank you for dancing to RPM and Balao Magico and for being the person I smoked my first cigarette with on the veranda of your bedroom after eating an entire lasagne Dona Luzia left for us when the family was out for the day (and commiserating with how terrible we felt afterward—I re-call that was the day you taught me how to say "stom-achache.") Thank you for showing me Rio de Janeiro and the majesty of Corcovado (Christ the Redeemer statue) and the miracles of the Convent of Nossa Senhora da Penha. Thank you for coming to experience what my life was like in Jacksonville and at MacMurray. Thank you for inviting me into your home, sharing time with your beautiful son, and taking us around to visit all the people and places I wanted to see that I missed. Thank you for remembering how much I love Serenata do Amor chocolates and having a whole bowl just for me. Thank you for all the late-night conversations in Portu-glish. Thank you for always mak-ing me "prova"- try it – something you often (sometimes bossily) urged me to do, to be adventurous. Thank you for leaving a piece of yourself in my heart, the piece that will always make me a little bit Brazilian.

And to all of my hosts who were strangers when I ar-rived in August, but had definitely become family by the time I left Brasil (with an s to those who live and love it there) that following July, thank you, I'm eternally grate-ful for and will always remember your kindness.

～

A LUCKY ENCOUNTER

My host families weren't the only "strangers" who showed me kindness that year; there was another who sticks out in my memory. One who appeared at just the right time, which felt like a guardian angel or a divine intervention.

Looking back today reminds me that everything happens for a reason.

At the end of my year abroad, as I was traveling home, my return flight was from Vitoria through Rio de Janeiro before arriving in the US. When I left, all of my family and friends came to see me off at the airport, and I could not stop sobbing at having to leave them, not knowing if I'd ever see them again. It felt so final after an amazing year, and I was still sniffling and clutching a bag of going-away gifts given to me there at the gate in Vitoria (the hardest to carry was a street sign) when I arrived at the Rio airport. This time, I was at least able to read the signs and communicate, so I felt more comfortable, that is until I checked in for my connecting flight back to the US. My stomach dropped and my mouth went suddenly dry when I discovered that I had to pay a tariff to leave the country. I had spent every last cruzeiro (the currency at the time) I had on souvenirs back in Vitoria. I asked the immigration guard what I could do, and he gruffly relayed that I had to come up with the money or I couldn't leave. And oh, by the way, he added that the flight was delayed and it would not be taking off for another four hours. I also had no money left to buy something to eat.

He dismissively told me to step out of line. I sat down in the closest row of seats, stunned and, once again, crying. What was I going to do? There were no ATMs then, and I didn't have a credit card. I had no way to call my parents, and my head started spinning with panic and desperation as I tried to figure out what to do. I was getting ready to call my Brazilian family, collect from a payphone, when a friendly-looking man in a polo shirt, cowboy hat and jeans approached me.

He quickly introduced himself, speaking in English as Joe, from Texas. He said he was behind me in line and overheard that I had a problem and asked about my situation. In between sobs, I confessed, probably all teenage angsty and dramatically, how I had spent the year studying and was trying to get home but didn't realize I had to pay to leave the country and that I had spent all of my money. He told me not to worry that he'd take care of it and make sure I got home. He got back in line with me and paid my fee to leave (it was around $70, which was no small fee then.) My passport and visa were stamped in approval, and I could go home!

But his kindness didn't stop there. He asked me if I had eaten dinner, and when I shook my head, embarrassed, he said with a Southern twang, "Well, I'm hungry; let's go get a bite to eat." First, he got a locker for me to stash my carry-on and bag of going-away gifts, noticing my struggle, especially with the street sign. What a relief I felt to not have to lug those around. We went to a sit-down restaurant where he asked the hostess to seat us next to a mother and her toddler son, whom he recognized and had apparently met earlier. He shared that she was visiting from Sweden and that she spoke fluent English, Swedish, German, and Portuguese, as did her 3-year-old son. I remember my amazement and awe at these world travelers, envious and hoping someday to be able to travel like them. During dinner, I learned that Joe lived in Texas near the border, and his mother had emigrated from Mexico. His life's work was helping to establish schools in poor towns over the border, collecting old office furniture from businesses, and arranging school supply drives to equip them with what they needed. Even as a teenager, I marveled not only at my luck in encountering this good Samaritan but in how he had dedicated his life to helping others in a way that felt so real and made an immediate difference.

At the end of the meal, we said our goodbyes to the mom and her amazingly multilingual son, who showed off his language knowledge by saying "goodbye" in all of them. Joe helped me collect and carry my belongings from the locker to the gate. He wished me well, and I thanked him again, but I never got his last name or thought to ask for his address. (In my defense, I was a 16-year-old kid excited to go home and see her family after a year.) He strode away without a backward glance, most likely off to help the next person he encountered. I would have loved to write him a thank you note, find out about his school-building projects, and maybe even support his efforts in the future. When I came home and told my parents, the first thing my mother asked was if I got his address to send him a proper thank you note. Nowadays, it might have been more along the lines of "How could you go off with a strange man in a foreign country," but I didn't give it a second thought—I trusted my instincts and his gentle, caring demeanor.

I have thought about Joe Last-Name-Unknown through the years: What happened to him? What other good did he go on to do? Was he married, did he have children, and were they continuing his mission? I still can't believe this immense kindness I received from a stranger. He was in the right place at the right time for me and provided exactly what I needed without asking for anything in return. I will never be able to thank him other than by paying it forward.

The experience of my year abroad shaped me and continues to have an influence on me today. It's the litmus test whenever I encounter a challenge. I say to myself, "Hey, if you can get on a plane at age 15 and go to a foreign country where you don't know a soul or speak the language for a year, you can do (whatever the challenge is—usually something involving public speaking)!" And during this season in my life, I learned I could do hard things—I could weather homesickness, a new culture, language barriers, all boosted through the kindness of strangers.

REFLECT AND CONNECT

Now it's your turn to reflect back on moments when a stranger's kindness had an impact...

- Think about a time that someone you didn't know showed up to help in a big or small way.
- What did they do and how did it change your outlook or circumstance at the time?
- How about when someone who started off as a stranger became a friend or even like family?
- What did they do that made you feel that way?

- Can you recall a time a stranger did something that made you feel hopeful or reminded you of our shared humanity?
- What was the gesture, and how can you pass it along?

Upon remembering these encounters, think how you can reach out and share. Let these former strangers know you remember what they did and that you are thankful for the role they played in that moment or in your life. Chances are they might not even realize it, and it may bring back some wonderful memories for them to reflect on as well.

If you are unable to contact them directly, like I cannot with Patricia and Joe, maybe you can reach out and share your memories and convey thanks to their families or friends, as I will with my Brazilian family. Their loved ones may be surprised and comforted to know how much they mattered to you and add a piece to their legacy, perhaps previously unknown.

"That strangers are friends that we some
day may meet" *–Edgar A. Guest*[5]

---

[5] Guest, Edgar Albert, "Faith," *The Light of Faith*, the Reilly & Lee Company, Chicago, 1926

CHAPTER 3

GRATEFUL FOR PARENTS

"There is no doubt that it is around the family and the home that all the greatest virtues... are created, strengthened and maintained."
—Winston Churchill[6]

I know that everyone's circumstances are different and that not everyone is close to their families. This makes me all the more appreciative of my parents and how they have always given us an unwavering sense of support, endless lessons learned, and a sense of belonging. From the very beginning of our lives, our parents take on the vast responsibility of bringing us into the world to care for us, of establishing us as a piece of a larger whole. It starts with bestowing a name upon us that gives us our identity and cements our being part of the family.

I've always rather liked my name, or the origin of my name; the fact that it was chosen after a book character, and I like that it's a derivative of Guinevere. What I don't

---

[6] As quoted in the following article: "Facing Uncertain Times: Rely on 'Family-First' Thinking." *DBRoot*, https://www.dbroot.com/resources/facing-uncertain-times-rely-on-family-first-thinking/. Accessed 9 Dec. 2024. While not a direct quote, it serves as a partial summation of the December 26, 1941 address to the US Congress by Churchill. It is commonly attributed to Churchill.

like about it is when that book became popular enough to make a movie out of that starred Ali MacGraw and Ryan O'Neal, my name became one of, if not the, most popular name and stayed that way for a decade. Also, I hope that the fact that the Jennifer in that book met a tragic end is not symbolic of my life. (Really, Mom, why would you name me after such a tragic character?) My middle name honors someone on both sides of the family: my paternal grandfather's sister and my maternal grandfather's mother. In an era where most middle names were Marie, Ann, Sue, or Lynn, I was glad I had a less common one, especially since my first name ended up being the title of a book for common names, *Beyond Jennifer and Jason.* In college I was one of three Jennifers, not in my dorm, or even on my floor, but on my wing of my floor- the Jenn with 2 N's became the differentiator, and it stuck.

~

"The mother's heart is the child's schoolroom."
—*Henry Ward Beecher*[7]

LOVE & CARE

Our mother is our first comforter, healer, cheerleader, protector, and teacher. We learn from her before we are even aware we are doing so by observing and absorbing. And with my Mom, there was a lot to observe; she always seemed to be busy. She was a working mom and always seemed on the go. When I was in elementary school,

---

[7] Beecher, Henry Ward. *Life Thoughts*. Phillips, Sampson and Company, 1858, p. 33.

I did not like that she wasn't home for us after school like a lot of my friends' moms were. I did not like that we could not go straight home after school. Instead, we had to walk to the babysitter's house across the street. When we started 3rd grade, we were deemed old enough to come straight home, let ourselves in, get a snack, and wait for her to come home. Now I can look back and realize how we were learning from her, as she managed a home and her work, caring deeply about both. I see that she was teaching us how to be responsible and easing us into being self-sufficient.

She was a kindergarten teacher in a low socioeconomic part of town, where the kids' meals, other than the free lunches, weren't necessarily guaranteed. She told us how many of the kids in her class would come to school without having had breakfast. I don't think the schools back then offered a breakfast option. On the mornings of the standardized statewide Iowa Basics testing, while we were scrambling to get ready in the morning, I remember Mom making sandwiches. She took time every one of those mornings to create an assembly line for making peanut butter and jelly sandwiches, spread across the entire countertop so she could take them to her students. She would buy the 15-cent milk cartons upon arriving at school, going in early to ensure she could pick up one for each of them. She'd then tote the blue plastic milk crate down to her room and place one on each desk next to the sandwiches in the folded tucked-in baggies (no Ziplocs yet) ready for their arrival so that "her kids" would start the day with their little bellies full instead of with an unfair disadvantage.

She truly cared for her students beyond just the year she had them in class. She told them all when they were in kindergarten that if they stayed in school and graduated from high school, she would be there to cheer them on at their graduation. She kept track of her students through the years and was true to her word. Every year, she would get dressed up and write a card for each former student before heading to "The Bowl" to watch and cheer them on as they crossed the stage. After the ceremony, she would seek out and personally congratulate each and every one of her former kindergartners who stuck with it and graduated. She was filled with pride for them.

Some of these students shared a special connection with her. They must have touched her on a different level. There was one little boy, Charles, whom she adored. She would come home and share stories of his classroom escapades. It was clear from the twinkle in her eye that his antics had captured a special place in her heart. He was from a family in town that was often in legal trouble, and I know she saw something in him and hoped he would not follow the same path. Another student touched her so deeply that she became her big sister through the Big Brother/Big Sister organization, which was our town's version of the Boys and Girls Club and remained so for many years. She could see and reflect back her potential when no one else did. She gave her a stable place to visit, a weekly warm bed that she didn't have to share, nice meals, and most importantly, 1:1 time where she was the sole focus, where someone would listen to her, her hopes and dreams, and struggles, amidst her life of being shuffled among the 14 foster homes throughout her childhood. Mom always believed in her and helped her to believe in her future. Years later, she helped her to write her college entrance essay and apply for financial aid.

I'm grateful to my mom for modeling how to connect with people, to look deeper and empathize and care for others. In high school I learned how her care for her young students stuck with them and how it cascaded, as I ended up being on the receiving end. During my sophomore year, I was having some bully issues. There was a group of girls who, if I ran into them in a bathroom, would circle round and pull my hair, take whatever money or pens or lip gloss were in my backpack, and threaten me if I told anyone. I was terrified of running into them, and it became a daily strategy for me to identify the bathrooms where I was more likely to run into them so that I could avoid them. One day, I was in a bathroom I thought was "safe" when they came out of the last stall, blowing smoke in my face, and started circling round. This time there was a new face. When she saw me, she asked, "Hey, is Mrs. Gay your mom?" I could only gulp and nod. The large girl with the wiry red hair and freckles broke out into a smile, and she told me Mrs. Gay was her kindergarten and favorite teacher. She told the group, "This is Mrs. Gay's daughter—leave her alone!" As they backed away, the tense atmosphere evaporated. The next semester she was in my gym class and claimed the locker across from mine so she could watch out for me. I no longer had to worry about which bathrooms were safe, and not only did the bullying stop, but I also now had a bodyguard in school and at off-campus school activities. Thanks, Mom.

> "Life doesn't come with a manual; it comes with a mother." —Unknown[8]

WHIMSICAL DETAILS

Growing up, Mom had a whimsical approach to everyday things that added fun and transformed the ordinary into magical moments. She had a way of making everything she created and presented feel special through her attention to the little details.

Throughout my childhood, we had a clown in our toilet. Yes, you read that right, a clown. When it came time to potty train my brothers standing up, she painted a little smiling clown face with nail polish in the toilet right above the water line to give them a place to aim (not sure what that says about how Mom feels about clowns...) The clown in our toilet was a fixture that we stopped noticing, but all of the guests who made a trip to the bathroom always commented on it. I remember hearing one of my parents' friends ask if they, too, were supposed to aim for the clown.

Her summer "breaks" were full of driving us and watching our sports. The three of us played in tennis

---

[8] https://jheconomics.com/life-doesnt-come-with-a-manual-it-comes-with-a-mother/

meets and tournaments, and she loaded up the station wagon and made sure we had gathered all of our needed equipment, had the directions or map (no GPS then), and off we would go—across the state, sometimes leaving before dawn to arrive when the tournaments started. I remember her complaining about a lot of things, namely us bickering, being messy, leaving things behind, but I don't ever remember one complaint about schlepping us from town to town. After we arrived, we checked in while she set up a comfortable "home base" for us with a blanket spread out, snacks in the picnic basket, and the generic Aldi brand of Kool-Aid (it was only 19 cents a pack, but you had to add your own sugar) in the spouted thermos for us. She usually found a prime spot under a tree and centrally located, but easy enough to move if we had to play on a far court. She was there to cheer us on.

Because Mom was always on the go, I would not describe her as a patient person, but she was uncharacteristically patient with us when we were sick. She gave us a bell to ring so that when we had a sore throat or stomach ache we didn't have to expend the energy to call out for her. She'd be able to hear the bell and respond according to the urgency of the ring and quickly be by our side. She'd appear with a little tray carrying soup and ice water, or saltines or graham crackers. Often, we could anticipate a little surprise such as a coloring book or puzzle to help us pass the time, as we did not have TVs in our bedrooms. It was all so nicely arranged, usually on a little towel, so that even when you felt miserable, you couldn't help but smile at her arrival, feeling loved and cared for.

And her cool hands were always a welcome feeling on a fevered forehead.

Lots of people laugh about the food they ate growing up. I've seen many posts and memes focusing on the food we ate in the 70s. But I look back with fond memories of my mom as a good cook, and although the food might not have been organic or fancy, it was always delicious. Meal time was family time, as we were expected to eat together around the table, whether we wanted to or not. One of my favorite childhood meals was reserved for the weekend—she would make a pot of Soup Starter with seasoned chunks of hamburger in it. After an afternoon of playing tag or kickball or raking leaves on a cold fall day, there was nothing better than coming into the toasty house with our pink, chilled cheeks and rumbling tummies to the smell of the Crock Pot full of soup with crackers or bread on the table. Another "special treat" was Mrs. Grass' soup. This soup came in a blue box that contained dry noodles, a seasoning packet, and a gold nugget, the prize of the box. My brothers and I would fight over who got to stand by Mom while she was making it and had the privilege of tossing the "gold nugget" into the pot, watching it dissolve. Simple dinners were made special through her presentation—grilled cheese sandwiches cut in little triangles and thoughtfully shaped on the plate with a designated place for the sides, alongside a little nest of chips, or carrot sticks and celery with a little pool of ranch salad dressing to dip them in. I admit that Mom went through an experimental health food kick in the late 70s, buying brown rice in bulk, and we were only allowed plain Cheerios and not the fun sugary cereal, but overall, the food of childhood reminds me of love and warmth as only a tuna noodle casserole with hand-crushed potato chips on top, made by Mom, can.

She just made events special. On the opening night of a summer play that I was in, for dessert, she surprised me with an ice cream sundae. It was presented in one of our blue swirl pedestal glass bowls reserved for special occasions. It was topped with a little triangular paper flag she had made out of a toothpick and written "Break a Leg!" on it. At first, I was horrified that she was wishing I'd break a bone, but she explained the saying. Then, I felt like I was in on the secret theater lingo. One New Year's Eve, she made fondue in our burnt orange enamel fondue pot, and we got to participate by choosing a color stick and cooking chopped up hot dogs in the hot oil.

Many kids in my town had their birthday parties at the roller rink or McDonald's or Pizza Hut. We didn't have the money for that, but Mom always made our birthdays and our parties memorable because they were creative. A couple in particular come to mind: a Junk Punk party where we only ate junk food, and my friends were asked to come dressed in punk attire, and a make-your-own-pizza party. The table was laid out with English muffins sliced in half and all of the toppings set out for our creations. She always led off with games that we enjoyed so much that I continued to play at my kids' parties. One of these was a memory game with objects she laid out on a tray (in this case, one of Dad's silver tennis trophy trays) and covered. She would remove the towel covering the objects with a flourish, and we'd have 60 seconds to observe and then recall and write down all we could remember. It was an annual tradition and a favorite. The best thing was that she wouldn't let me see the objects ahead of time so that I could play too. And on our birthday, she made us construction paper crowns, stapled together, and warm fuzzies to wear (a happy face made out of leftover shaggy bathroom carpeting with black construction paper eyes and a big smile stuck on with rolled masking tape), and we always got to choose the meal she made for our dinner and our favorite flavor of Pepperidge Farm cake.

Looking back, I am thankful for the example she set and for teaching me how to care for others, how to have fun, how to pay attention to the details, and how those details make a difference because they make people feel special. She continues to teach and pass on these lessons: her knowledge of cooking, sheet folding, outfit compiling, manners and etiquette, school challenges, and parenting. And I love watching her teach her grandkids. When my kids were learning colors, she proclaimed a whole day as Yellow Day—where they noticed and shared and drew and ate everything yellow (yellow sun, yellow school bus, yellow crackers, etc.) She has a gift for reaching children just where they are, making activities fun, and making the experience special. Thanks again, Mom, for a life of lessons and love.

"A father is someone you look up to no matter how tall you grow." —Unknown[9]

ULTIMATE PROVIDER

For many, our father is our first role model, first advisor, and for some daughters, definitely true for me, the first man we love. We watch and see how they protect us and provide for the family. When we are young, we literally look up to them in awe and amazement. And then, as they are often also our first disciplinarian, a respectable level of fear creeps in when we hear the familiar threat: "Wait until your father gets home!" I can remember getting spanked as a young child a total of two times (fewer than my brothers for sure), and that was enough for me.

As kids, you know who to go to when you need something, even if you get in trouble for going to one, hear a no, and then "just check" with the other. My parents are the best complement to each other: Mom's emotional side is balanced by Dad's logic; Mom's energy is balanced by Dad's calming presence. We knew to go see Dad when we needed to calm down or needed a non-emotional viewpoint or logical advice on something, being the loving, supportive and the ultimate provider that he is.

Dad worked year-round. During the school year, he was a professor, coach, and later the athletic director, and then he spent his summers off school as the tennis pro at the local country club. One of the perks he con-

---

[9] https://hoorayheroes.com/stories/25-fathers-day-quotes-to-make-dad-feel-the-love/

sidered when taking the job was the fact that we'd be able to go to the club each day too. We were able to join the swim and tennis teams, which was where my brothers and I learned to swim. We would spend our entire days out at the club with Dad - going out with him early in the morning before the ladies' leagues started, helping him open up the tennis shack, raising the nets and filling up the water coolers, not heading for home until the men's after-work leagues started. Playing tennis and swimming from morning to evening was a fun way to improve our games, spend time with him, and be with friends. In addition to his running tennis team practices in the late mornings after the leagues ended, he gave lessons—group and private. He was out in the sun all day but would never say no if we asked him to hit the ball with us. He'd take the basket out, set it up behind the net on the opposite side, and hit us baskets of balls. The only rule was we had to pick them up, although he would always help. I still am amazed at the precision with which he could hit those to us, at exactly the right place, every time. In the evenings, while watching the Cub games, he'd string rackets for extra money and sometimes would even give lessons to folks in the community after dinner. And every Sunday morning, he went down to the IGA to get us donuts, a special treat to end the week.

During the school year, when he'd come home after basketball practice in the evenings and after dinner, he would have papers to grade which he could do even if we were running around with the TV blaring or fighting with each other. He had tremendous focus and could tune out anything, much to my mother's dismay—she'd ask a question, and he truly wouldn't hear. It was not selective hearing, as best we know. Through the years, he was offered other coaching and teaching positions at bigger schools, far more prestigious than his small private liberal arts school, but he stayed there for what I think are a couple of reasons: first, he graduated from the college and was mentored there by his former coach. I think he had a true love and loyalty to the school, a history which made it feel like home. And second was because, as a professor there, his kids were able to go to college there (and later at some exchange schools) tuition-free. What he didn't make in salary, he definitely made up for in perks, and he chose to do this so that he could give his kids a college education, one where we did not have to start our young adult lives worried about paying back tuition loans. I appreciated this when I was in college, but I appreciate it even more now as an adult with kids in college myself.

Dad would go out of his way to do something for us, even if it meant it was outside his comfort zone—things like going into Front Row Records, and when he couldn't find the cassette I asked for, going up to the clerk for help to find the tape by the band who sang the Egyptian song. "You know, The Bagels?" only to be asked, "You mean the Bangles?"

ADVISOR AND COACH

Dad was well known in town, often interviewed and quoted in the newspaper after games. In the summer, he was known for his tennis. In addition to leading the tennis team and giving lessons, he played in a lot of tennis tournaments. He would almost always make it to the final matches and often won. We had a lot of trophies and silver platters in our house from his victories. It was fun for us to watch him, both because he was our dad but because he was a great player. We learned a lot by watching him, and he'd review key points with us after the matches. I admired the way he played, how he didn't give up and could move on the court and get to so many of the shots. He never lost his temper—sportsmanship was a huge thing to him, and although he hated losing probably more than most with his natural competitive fire, he did not lose his composure. Ours was definitely a competitive household between him and my two athletic brothers. How could some of that not rub off on me? But sportsmanship was something he stressed—he would not tolerate poor sportsmanship, no matter how many other kids were throwing their rackets or shouting. We knew if we pulled any stunt like that, we'd be yanked off the court so fast our heads would spin.

His face would be the one I'd look for on the sidelines when I was playing. He could give me advice without saying a word. I would be looking for approval or for hints at where I was going wrong—slow down, quicken the feet, play to the left/the right, go up, throw the ball higher. I knew by his look and sometimes his motions what to try doing more of, always seeking his coaching.

Dad spent hours with us on the tennis court, jogging with us to improve our conditioning and shooting hoops and throwing baseballs with my brothers. During these activities, we had a lot of our conversations, the serious talks, and heart-to-hearts. Another time I would frequently seek his advice would be at night when we'd watch the old *Leave it to Beaver* reruns together after the 10 pm news ended. Many times, during commercial breaks, I'd ask questions or tell him what was on my mind, and he'd share his perspective or what he'd recommend. It felt like a safe space that was just ours.

I remember one summer at the club, he wouldn't allow me to move up on the tennis ladder even though I had beat the person who was ranked above me. She and I were pretty evenly matched and went back and forth a lot, but he chose the other girl over me to play in the spot I wanted for an important match. I was angry and asked him about it, saying it wasn't fair because he knew more than anyone else how hard I'd been practicing and that I'd actually won this time. He explained that I could not be considered higher than the members' kids there, that it may appear that he was playing favorites, and he just would not do that. It still felt unfair to me, but I didn't want him to get in trouble or lose his job. I understood why he made the choice. He praised me for how hard I had been working on conditioning and practicing serves and that certainly lessened the sting.

He started a tradition of spending focused 1:1 time with us before home basketball games. I always looked forward to the days when it was my turn. Mom would drop us off at his office after school, and he'd let us choose where to go for dinner. My favorite was always the Wendy's salad bar- it was enormous, and they had so many things to choose from. They also had the best blue cheese dressing, something Dad always had too, and we had that in common. Then we'd go to the gym, and I'd get to choose to either sit on one of the chairs next to the players during the game or with the fans in the stands. My brothers liked sitting by him, I preferred to sit across where I could also watch the cheerleaders and the half-time show. I wasn't so into the games, but I liked the special time with Dad, where he asked about my day, activities of the time, listening, connecting, and often offering advice on whatever challenges I was facing those days be that friendship, schoolwork or sports-related.

Dad and I had a period of time when I was in high school where we just did not relate to each other. I think he didn't know what to make of me when I returned from Brazil, 30 pounds heavier, with bleached hair, six earrings, and wearing fishnets. We used to go for family dinners at Pizzans Pizza for family night each week—it was a weekly Wednesday night ritual: a large pizza (and I can honestly say I've never found an equal to that pizza of my childhood), a pitcher of Coke and four quarters for the arcade games. We each got one quarter and then the extra got rotated each week. This had been a family tradition for a long while, but after I got back from Brazil,

I don't think my family, my dad in particular, really liked being seen with me in public. I was just too weird for a conservative town with the way I now looked and people stared. I suspect the staring made him uncomfortable. Sometimes, they left for Pizzans before I got home from after-school activities. Other times, I sensed they were embarrassed and let them go without me, making some excuse or just asking them to bring me home a slice or two.

Things turned around for us, though, when I was in college. My freshman year, I went to school out of state rather than the college in my hometown. I needed to get out of town, but I soon realized I didn't feel the ties like I did to that school. I ended up transferring my sophomore year back to the college on the campus where I grew up. In retrospect, I think that I mellowed a bit, became a little less "out there," a little more traditional in the way I looked and dressed. I stopped dying my hair so often. From time to time, I would see Dad walking from one building to the next on the way to classes, and I made at least a couple of visits to his office each week. One time in particular, I was upset over boy troubles and went into his office and started crying. I'm not much of a crier, so it was unusual for him to see. He immediately shut the office door, gave me a huge hug, and some very typical but reassuring advice along the lines of plenty of fish in the sea, not being in a hurry to find love, and just focusing on schoolwork. I remember he said he wanted me to go pick out something to cheer me up and gave me some money. When I tried not to take it, he insisted

I find a little something. That meant a lot to me, and so I was careful about what I chose—an Esprit t-shirt with a little French cafe scene that I loved. I had that shirt for years. When it got stained at the bottom, I cut it off and made it a "half shirt" because every time I wore it, I remembered how he had comforted me. That shirt was like a Dad hug.

It was also in college when I saw how his counsel and advice went beyond the walls of our home to others. This realization came through seeing the influence he had on the students he taught and the players he coached. And it really hit me when a friend told me how helpful he had been in giving her and a friend advice when they went to him with a personal problem. I was astonished by his open-mindedness and deeply proud that he was the person they sought advice from. How lucky I was to have him as my dad.

One of the toughest things I find about my dad's illness is making decisions with my family around what is best for him. It's hard because I have never made an important decision without first consulting him and getting his perspective and advice. He has always listened to our dilemmas and walked us through the pros and cons of each decision, helping us to reach our own conclusions, and advising us whether that be a decision about our homes, jobs, money, or matters of the heart.

I recently asked my brothers to give me a few words they felt described Dad, and this is the list: competitive, passionate, intelligent, logical, understanding, humble, calming, and approachable—I couldn't agree more. Thank you, Dad, for always being there, protecting and providing for us, for your patience and your wise counsel.

~

REFLECT AND CONNECT

When thinking about your parents or the parental figures in your life:

- What are some of the traits you remember and appreciate in them?
- What are some of the positive qualities or gifts they modeled through their actions that they might not have been aware of?
- Are there qualities of theirs you see in yourself, your siblings, or passed down to your children?
- What are the adjectives you would use to describe your mother or mother figure? How about your father or father figure?
- What special practices, customs, or traditions do you remember from your childhood? What, as an adult, do you look back and appreciate most about these events?
- If you could choose one thing to thank them for, what would that be? Has this changed over the years?
- What do you realize now about them that you didn't years ago? I suggest that you share that one first.

- If they are grandparents, what do you see in them as grandparents that you didn't notice in them as parents?
- Share with your parents what makes you proud of them or of being their child.

I urge you to reach out to your parents and share some of your memories and reasons you are grateful to them. If they are no longer here, please share them with your family members or friends of theirs with whom you keep in touch so they can remember and reflect with you. Let them know how these memories have impacted you, shifted your perspective, or even helped shape the way you parent.

—— CHAPTER 4 ——

GRATEFUL FOR SIBLINGS

"To the outside world, we all grow old. But not to
brothers and sisters. We know each other as we
always were, we know each other's hearts, we share
private family jokes. We remember family feuds
and secrets, family griefs and joys."
– *Clara Ortega*[10]

The sibling relationship is something special. As we grow, we see less and less of the carefree childhood siblings we once knew. We can still catch glimpses of their former selves in how they interact with their children or nieces and nephews, and it is such a gift. Throughout childhood, we fight with them, celebrate with them, experiment with them (pouring water down the hurricane of a lit lamp, not one of our greatest ideas); we create our own adventures with them, and we turn to them in times of need. They are our first playmates and the ones we test boundaries and get into trouble with. They see us when we are at our best—helping us celebrate our wins in the classroom, on the court, in a social circle, on the stage, because they saw how

---

[10] Zúñiga Ortega, Clara Luz. *José María Arguedas: Un Hombre Entre Dos Mundos*. Fondo Editorial de la Pontificia Universidad Católica del Perú, 1994.

hard we worked and practiced. And they see us at our worst—our tantrums, being sent to our rooms, illnesses, being grounded, or embarrassed. But they are the few who actually see our true selves during our formative years growing up in a way that outsiders cannot, and that creates an immeasurable bond, one that is evident when someone else tries to say something bad about them. That family loyalty gene kicks in, and it's fierce.

I loved the novelty of having sisters while living abroad with host families, but I've always been thankful for being the only girl in the family, and I loved having brothers even more. As the oldest of three, I've been told I was always the little mother hen, which eventually became the nickname given to me by my youngest brother, "Jenn the Hen," and I have to admit it's pretty fitting. In not having sisters to compete with and being separated by a few years, I can honestly say I don't remember there ever being any sibling rivalry between us. I was excited to have brothers and playmates after having only my imaginary friends, Herschel and Gunka, for the first three years of my life. And I never delighted in my brothers' being punished like a lot of siblings do. Quite the opposite, it hurt me when they got in trouble. And this was something I experienced frequently, as one brother in particular got in trouble often—definitely more than both the other and I combined.

⁓

"Family is not an important thing. It's everything."
—Michael J. Fox

MIDDLE BROTHER

My brother Jonathan was also named after a book, a sweet little story called Jonathan Livingston Seagull. Like the seagull, he has always strived to live life to the fullest, challenge boundaries, and forge his own path.

Jonathan is three years younger than me, and in the early days, I think he went along with whatever I wanted to do, but that was short-lived. During the 70s, when couples were taking disco dancing lessons, he became my partner when our parents came home and showed us their "latest moves." We would be doing the Bus Stop alongside them in the living room, laughing as we tried to follow along. Later, we graduated to putting on our own dance shows. Ross and Monica's dance routine in Friends was something I related to, even though ours were only performed in the comfort of our home and not in front of a television audience. We watched the old-school Adam West Batman together and loved acting out the fight scenes along with Batman and Robin's KaPOW! We were watching Batman when my dad came home with a surprise for my brother.

There was a blow-up airplane that hung in the Party House, a liquor store adjacent to the grocery store. I don't think there was much of a selection back then in the grocery store, so we'd tag along with Dad when he'd go to pick up a 6-pack of beer or bottle of wine. I always wanted to go along in hopes that I could talk Dad into a Marathon candy bar or pack of gum when we reached the counter. Jonathan's motivation for going was seeing that plane. The plastic blow-up airplane was about three feet long with the same size wingspan. It hung in one of the aisles, suspended on a string from the ceiling tiles. It was there for a couple of years, and every time we were lucky enough to join Dad, he'd go right to that aisle and stand underneath, marveling at that plane. And then suddenly, it was gone, no longer "flying" over the aisle, and he was distraught about it, asking where it went and why it had to go away, telling Mom that the plane was gone as soon as we got home.

A few weeks after the plane disappeared, Dad came home with a box for Jonathan. When he opened it up, there was the deflated plane. The lady manager at the Party House with the red jacket, dyed dark hair, gravelly voice, and friendly smile had apparently noticed his love for the plane and how he sought it out any time he was in the store. When it was taken down, she had saved it behind the counter for the next time Dad was in. Dad quickly blew it up for him. That airplane was loved as much at home as it was in the Party House. In retrospect, it probably wasn't a great "toy" to play with, I think it was an ad for Seagrams or some other liquor. But that goes to show how the community is in a small town—people notice you and remember you and I know Jonathan was thrilled.

Jonathan and I have shared a lot, including suffering through chicken pox. Our youngest brother had them first, and then exactly 14 days later, we both had "the pox" appear. We were so itchy with our only relief being Aveeno baths. I recently found the pictures from that time—we were both completely covered, but at least we had someone to commiserate with. He was there to share my excitement at the first record I bought, Supertramp It's *Raining Again*, and would share his own with me through the years. One year, he even got one "for me" for Christmas, knowing full well that *Breakin' 2: Electric Boogaloo* wasn't something I would be into and would let him listen to it, maybe even I'd let him just keep it in his room.

Jonathan had a little strut in the way he walked, kind of on his tiptoes but definitely with an air of "here I come, don't mess with me." He was one of the best tennis players growing up: strong, athletic, and a bit of a daredevil. He would not give up; he had a mental toughness and competitiveness that I respected, something that he and Dad had in common and bonded over. Long after I'd lost and been eliminated from one of the many tennis tournaments of our summers, he would often go on to the final rounds. I remember feeling so proud that he was my brother and was excited to watch him play; he was such a competitor. He never let the stress or pressure get to him. If he made it to the finals, chances were pretty good he was going to win.

I never had to worry about him holding his own with neighborhood kids or bullies at school. He was a little mouthy and unafraid, and people didn't mess with him. I was always actually more afraid of him getting hurt than anything because of his daring demeanor. One time, he fell off the top of a van after crawling up while our friend's mom had stopped and didn't realize he had climbed up the back ladder as she had pulled over to the curb and was in a conversation with our mom. He wanted to try out car surfing and ended up trying out getting stitches in his head instead. Another time, he went flying down our hill of a street on his bike no-handed. We lived at the top (our house was #1), and he picked up pace as he went down and ended up flipping over the handlebars. As my mother put it, he "cleaned up the street with his face." Thankfully, he had no permanent scars, but it was a bloody, scabby mess, and I never rode no-handed after seeing what happened to him. But he was not afraid of what most kids were— his only fears were dogs and that Jaws was lurking in Lake Jacksonville.

He and my mother pushed each other's buttons the whole time we were growing up. I don't know if it was because they had similar temperaments, or that they both liked having the last word, or whether he just got a charge out of talking back. But he and Mom would get into it, and she would usually call his bluff. I remember one time when we were really young and grocery shopping, he was begging for something, most likely candy or a toy, and Mom said no. He pulled out all the stops and started wailing with a full-on tantrum on the floor, kicking and pounding his little fists, thinking she'd give in. Instead, she told him to stop, or she would leave. When he did not stop, she grabbed my hand and led me away. I remember looking back over my shoulder and seeing him on the floor and the scared disbelief I felt that she would leave him. She said he would learn his lesson and stop and come find us. We went over a few aisles, and I could still hear him carrying on. And then, pretty quickly, when he realized he had lost his audience, it stopped. I went back to where he was and peered around the end of the aisle. He was still there, in the toy aisle, focused intently on the toys on the shelves, not a care in the world of where we were or that he was left behind. Mom was right, but I don't think you could do something like that today.

Sometimes, he would threaten to run away when he got into it with Mom. One time, he did. He packed a bag (probably with baseball cards and a snack) and walked off, cutting across the lawn of the house opposite ours and disappearing a couple streets down. I was scared that he wasn't going to come back and especially worried he wouldn't come home before dinner or before it got dark. I wondered, *Where will he sleep? What will he eat?* "Oh, he'll be back before dinner," Mom said. He was gone for maybe a half hour. We later found out he had been hiding in a bush, only two streets over, waiting it out, just sure he was making my mom worry. He was showing her. He stayed until the owner of the house let the dog out, who found him and chased him out of the yard, barking. He ran all the way home. He may have returned with his tail between his legs, but I was relieved he was safe and home in time for dinner.

His sense of humor has always been a bit on the wry side, often pulling pranks, some that weren't immediately evident. I remember another trip to the Eagles grocery store, and my mom standing in the checkout line under the fluorescent lights, taking her checkbook out and opening it up on the little pedestal to write it out. I loved watching her write checks and couldn't wait to be a grown-up so I could someday write checks and sign my name like I was famous. And then my mom was asked for her ID. I saw the surprise on her face when she saw her picture had been enhanced with a black sharpie mustache and the embarrassment as she explained to the cashier how her son must have done that. Next, disappointment crossed her face as she likely realized she was stuck with this version of her license until it was time to renew.

I remember when I got back from Brazil how much he had changed in one year—his voice was deep, he had probably grown a foot. He looked more like a man than my little brother, the one I had left behind a year ago. For my high school graduation the next year, he gave me a stone Fossil watch that he chose himself. I was touched that he had spent his own money and picked out such a cool gift, one that seemed grown up and lasting. I was not around for his high school years, so I missed the direct experience of what I suspect are some of his "best stories." Some live on in legend and are retold when we get together with childhood friends.

I feel so lucky to have the brothers I have. I'm grateful for our history and the 50+ years of antics and smiles. And I revel in the fact that he still pulls the little pranks that make me laugh. Just last week, Mom told me that she went into her planner and noticed someone had written "poop" on her calendar for that day. She immediately asked my nephew who was visiting if he did that, and he said, "No, Mimi, but I saw Uncle Jon go in your room." Mystery solved.

Thank you, Jonathan, for the years of friendship and support, for the shared experiences of our childhood, for the laughs, and for my special graduation gift. I still have that watch, and it still works.

~

"They say that no matter how old you become, when you are with your siblings, you revert back to childhood." – *Karen White*[11]

LITTLE BROTHER

By the time my youngest brother joined the family, since we already had two J names, our parents wanted to follow suit. They had two potential names they proposed, and they let us choose: Jason or Jeremy. Jon and I chose Jeremy and, looking back, I'm happy that my 5-year-old self chose well. He is not a Jason; he is definitely a Jeremy, and we didn't need two of the most common names in the family. Interestingly, Jeremy is the one child in the family not named for a book, and he is the one who is not a big reader. Jon and I are. Jeremy's middle name honors my great-grandfather, someone who loved yard work and took great pride in his lawn and garden. Jeremy has always been an outdoor person. Even when he was young, he didn't mind yard work. And today, he spends most, if not all, weekends in the yard. I wonder if the

---

[11] White, Karen. *The Memory of Water*. NAL Trade, 2008.

name chosen for us somehow foretells or influences the person we become.

Jeremy was pretty easygoing from the get-go and tagged along everywhere we went, to our many swim and tennis meets and soccer games until he was old enough to play too. As a toddler especially, he always seemed to have a runny nose and had the tendency to whine, often. We found out why after a Fourth of July I will always remember. In fact, I think about it every year.

This particular year, in the late 70s, we started noticing that Jeremy wasn't hearing well. I remember the "test" Dad devised that confirmed this. Jeremy was sitting under the table, and Dad asked him if he wanted a piece of candy. Jeremy didn't react. He was a child who could not resist his sweets, and we knew he would've jumped at the chance to eat candy if he'd heard the offer. Mom got a referral to the nearest audiologist, who was located in Quincy (about an hour and a half away). They determined Jeremy needed surgery to have tubes put in his ears, which was novel at the time, but we were told it would help with the achy ears and runny nose. He was scheduled for that surgery later that summer.

The annual traditions of the July 4th celebration at the club included a day filled with games both on the tennis courts and in the pool. One favorite was a coin dive, where we all sat on the edge of the pool with our eyes closed, waiting for the coaches to throw the coins in. Hearing the plink and clunk of them as they hit the water, our anticipation grew with each sound. When the whistle blew, we dove in to scoop up as many as we could, the coveted new bicentennial quarters being the most sought after and the ones responsible for that clunking sound.

Another favorite was "Beat the Pros," where Dad and Mr. Fredericks, the swim coach, would play a doubles game against two kids at a time- but with a twist- they'd play with frying pans instead of tennis rackets, and if the kids beat them, they got a prize. I remember waiting impatiently, hopping up and down for my turn in the line at the side of the court. The prizes we got to choose from if we won a game were amazing. I was always on the lookout for something called Super Elastic Bubble Plastic— that plasticky scent and the swirling colors were magical. If you blew in the straw just right, bubbles emerged that wouldn't pop—you could touch them and toss them around like a balloon as long as you kept them off the grass. The day's events ended with the fireworks.

Fireworks were set off by the local firefighters over the lake at the public park, and we could see the display from the club golf course across the lake. It was an anticipated way to end a day that had been filled with nothing but fun: lying on the blankets with friends and family, watching the fireworks overhead, goofing around, sharing secrets, playing chase with the booming light display, and the chorus of oohs and ahhs at the most spectacular ones.

Partway through the fireworks display this year, though, someone noticed that Jeremy wasn't with his normal buddy, Christie. My parents called out to the nearby groups to ask, but no one had seen him for a while. It was pitch dark, except for the occasional and momentary firework-lit sky, so the families who were with us all joined in trying to find him, calling out and searching for Jeremy. The realization that he wasn't going to be able to hear us well only increased the urgency and, for me, the fear factor. I was too afraid to wander off and look, and we were told to stick with someone and not go far. All I could do was wonder and worry. Parents were spreading out (remember, this was before we had flashlights on our phones, and I doubt anyone had a flashlight with them) to cover the course in different directions. Adults would check certain holes and return back with their report... no luck. He was lost. I remember the fear growing each time someone would report in, unsuccessful in locating my brother. By this time, the fireworks had finished, and people were packing up and leaving. I could see that my parents and the other adults were panicking, which was making me more scared. My mom was frantically asking people as they passed by on their way to their cars if they had seen him, and Dad was part of the search party looking for him.

It was the first time I remember being scared that someone I loved might die. In my 8-year-old view, it was logical: He was missing, he couldn't hear, he couldn't swim, he was alone, and it was dark. Eventually, a teenage family friend, Scott, found him down at the last hole before the lake, under a tree, crying. He had been shouting out his name but did not get a response and found him solely because he heard his sobs. When Scott returned with him, there were hugs all around, both for Jeremy and his safe return and for Scott, who, to me, seemed like a hero. I had never been so happy to see Jeremy or appreciated someone's help so much.

Jeremy was so young that he doesn't remember the incident, which seemed like it dragged on forever. Recently, I asked my mom how long he was missing, and she said it was about an hour. I was so thankful that he was okay, and I don't think I let go of his hand in the back seat the whole car ride home. We were all now looking forward to the surgery so he'd be able to hear.

As he grew and became more interactive, Jonathan and I played less often, and he and Jeremy were together all of the time, especially since they shared a bedroom. Jonathan was learning that he now had someone younger and that he could make the rules. When he would do something Jeremy didn't like, which seemed to be constantly, Jeremy would tattle. He also could not keep a secret. We learned that we couldn't tell him anything, especially anything to do with surprises or presents. When we'd wrap birthday gifts for my dad, my dad looked at the wrapped gift and jokingly said, "I wonder what's in here?" Jeremy would shout out, "It's tennis balls, Dad!" or "It's peanuts!" Many surprises were ruined in those days by Jeremy's over-eager mouth. Thankfully, he grew out of this stage, and his kids don't seem to have inherited the blabbermouth gene.

As Jeremy got older, he focused his attention on his outfits. He wanted to be perfectly matched—his sweatbands had to match the tennis shorts or shirt. There are quite a few pictures of him in his youth, not only with his wristbands matching his shirt and shorts but also with a matching headband! His nickname for a while became Fashion Plate, after one of my Christmas toys where you could combine and design and color outfits. He was the one in the family who noticed and desired name brands and asked for specific clothes. He especially loved shoes (and still does) and often requested that Mom take him to his favorite store, Shoe Carnival. While my allowance went to books and pens, and Jonathan's to baseball cards, Jeremy's most often went to the latest fashion fads.

I remember him saying once that he identified with the show *The Wonder Years*, and that was an interesting perspective to me. He said, like Kevin, he too had a weird older sister and a bully for a big brother, and he was, of course, the normal, sweet one. I can see it.

I was not around for his high school years either, and the closeness we shared from our everyday childhood experiences faded, as it does when you leave home. I am thankful that I was able to get to know him again later when he was in college and lived with me for a summer while he had an internship where I worked. I was proud to show him off as my brother and watch how he interacted and made friends and good impressions. He has always been and continues to be a genuine, likable, easygoing guy who can talk to anyone, and I continue to be impressed by this. We had our routine of stopping in the morning at White Hen Pantry for a fountain coke and riding bikes in the Forest Preserve after work. I was grateful for being able to get to know him, for the person he had grown to be and for that experience of being able to share a workplace and workplace friends, away from home.

After he graduated from college, he moved out west for a bit. During that time, he sent me a letter that included some musings and reflections on us, what made us who we were, how he noticed we felt more deeply, noticed and appreciated our surroundings, and how lucky we were to have our family. He enclosed some artsy black and white photos that he'd taken, knowing that I loved them, of him and Red Rocks Canyon and talked about some of the adventures he was having. I kept that letter for years and would look back and reread it from time to time as it reminded me how grateful I was for him, for his perspective on our family, and learning it was a sentiment we shared.

Jonathan once said that we had won the womb lottery. That, although we could have been born in any country to any set of parents, we were born into ours. This is a reflection that I often think of. Through the years, my brothers have supported me in every way, and I look back with a deep appreciation for the memories, the history, the loyalty, the laughs, and for how close we are. I love you, little brothers.

REFLECT AND CONNECT

Think about your siblings, those you grew up with, or those in your life who have felt like siblings and some of the memories you have...

- What is something you and your sibling(s) played regularly as kids?
- When did a sibling help you see things in a different way?
- What is a lesson they taught you or that you learned together?
- When did they stick up for you or have your back?
- Was there a time when you were afraid for them? What do you remember from that time?
- What traits do you think of when you think of them? Have these changed or stayed the same since childhood?
- Do you have childhood nicknames that haven't been used in a while? Is it about time to resurrect them?
- What is something you planned together that led to getting in trouble? Who got in the most trouble, and what did you learn from that "adventure"?

Think about some of the ridiculous experiences you've had, the goofy things you've done, shows or games you used to watch or play. Reach out to them and remind them about these—it will probably result in a smile or at least a solid smirk.

CHAPTER 5

GRATEFUL FOR FAMILY

"Ohana means family and family means nobody
gets left behind or forgotten." – *Stitch*[12]

OUR FAMILY BRANCHES

When I envision my family tree, I first see the main trunk
and branches of the immediate members. I sometimes
forget that we are part of a bigger picture. When you
step back and look at it from further away and take it all
in, it's a different view. A view that is far more interesting
and that encompasses our whole being. It's not just how
those close-by branches helped form us and made us
grow, but how the roots and the branches a little further
away also nourish us, helping us thrive and grow and
giving us the collective strength to withstand storms.

I didn't grow up with extended family close by. I was
envious of people who had a lot of cousins around who
were in and out of their family houses and aunts and uncles who were part of their everyday life. We lived four
hours away from both sets of grandparents, and my aunts
and uncles moved around all over—Eastern seashore,

---

[12] *Lilo and Stitch*. Directed by Dean DeBlois and Chris Sanders, Walt Disney
Animation Studios, 2002

Washington state, the Southwest, other countries, literally everywhere. On the rare occasions when we did get together, it was a special time, and there are some things about my family that, upon looking back and reflecting, I'm very proud of. One of them is the military history on both sides of the family.

Several of my family members served in the military, and I am fortunate that none lost their lives in doing so. Both of my grandfathers and one of my uncles were in the Navy, and my aunt and uncle actually met while serving in the Air Force. Tracing old stories and genealogy through Ancestry, etc. I have discovered that most of my relatives were in the military, and I feel a deep sense of pride and gratitude about that. I don't know much about their experiences or how they felt about their service, and this is something I wish I would've captured when I had the chance to ask them about it. I do know that my grandfather was away in World War II and did not meet my mother until she was about 18 months old. My grandmother was a young mother, renting a room outside of Chicago on a turkey farm. The farmer and his wife helped her navigate being a new mother, waiting for letters to arrive from her husband, looking forward to the day when she would be reunited with him and he would meet his daughter, my mother. She was named after him (Robert/Roberta), and the story is that when she finally did meet him, she was scared of his scratchy beard and howled as he picked her up from her playpen.

But other than snippets I've heard through the years, I don't know my family members' stories, what urged their bravery in putting their country before themselves, what they learned through serving—and I'd like to know. I have seen photos of some family members in uniform, and I plan to talk to my living relatives about their service. I think it's especially important to recognize, talk about, honor, and appreciate them for that. We enjoy freedoms today because of those who bravely came before us. We don't say it enough in our family, but to Aunt Kyle, Uncle Steve, Uncle Roger, and to both of my grandfathers, thank you for your service—please know how much you are appreciated and how proud your family is of you.

"The family is the first essential cell of human society." – *Pope John XXIII*[13]

PATERNAL BRANCHES

When I think about the paternal branches of my family tree, especially my dad's brothers, what immediately comes to mind is how competitive they were with each other. We did not get together often, but when we did, it involved family trips, and they were exciting, something we looked forward to and talked about for months. Usually, these get-togethers were planned around an event—a wedding or a family reunion. We would drive from Illinois to Delaware or to North Carolina to stay with one of my uncles' families. These vacations were lively because the whole family was there, and there was

---

[13] John XXIII. *Pacem in Terris: Encyclical of Pope John XXIII on Establishing Universal Peace in Truth, Justice, Charity, and Liberty.* 11 Apr. 1963.

a lot of catching up and reconnection with our cousins whom we hadn't seen for several years. These trips bustled with cookouts and games, swimming and playing tennis, and golf matches for the guys. We kids loved the junk food and the soda pop that was set out, unmonitored, that we were allowed at these events, and everything else that comes along with a family party, like later bedtimes. Grandma was in her element, the look of contentment, of satisfaction, and pride at watching her boys and their families, everyone all together.

The daytime activities varied, but the evenings usually involved Euchre tournaments. And the competition between the brothers during those card games was fierce. After sitting in as the 4th player one time and realizing very quickly I could not keep up with their level of play, my partner muttering under his breath after I played a card, I learned to steer clear of the back porch or family room where the card table was set up. They took their games very seriously, voices were raised and it was easy to imagine the three brothers as kids, fighting over who was the best, the smartest, the coolest.

I also remember how my uncles showed an interest in me. Both of them would inevitably pull me aside at some point during the vacation to learn about current interests, activities, hobbies: How are your grades? What is your favorite subject? Do you have a boyfriend? How is tennis going? It was in these moments I felt connected, no matter how long it had been since I'd seen them. I didn't realize these moments were important to them, too, until I received one of the most touching letters from my Uncle Steve. Upon my high school graduation, which my uncles were unable to attend, I received a handwritten letter on a sheet of yellow legal paper. Uncle Steve, who generally was not very demonstrative or affectionate, wrote a surprisingly sentimental letter telling me how sad he was that he wasn't able to be there to witness my accomplishments over the years in person. He wanted me to know that he was always cheering me on, and excited to hear about what I was up to, and that he was proud of me. He shared that he wished we were able to see each other more often. It was such a heartfelt letter that meant so much to me. I saved that letter in its envelope for many years in my box of keepsakes, rereading it to relish in the words and sentiments. Uncle Steve is gone now, and I wish I still had that letter to share it with his kids, so they can see an example of how their father had an influence from afar. I appreciate that he took the time to tell me things that I didn't previously know. It was a surprise to me, one that made me feel loved.

One summer when I was in college, I had an internship in Washington, DC. I shared an apartment with three other interns. I had to learn to navigate the multiple legs of public transportation to reach downtown each day. I had to learn to buy and make my own food, which was a new experience for me. All of the roommates were over 21, so they would go out on weekends together, and I, as the youngster, had to stay behind. I felt rather lonely that summer.

One night, one of the roommates told me I had a call. It was my Uncle Steve from Delaware, inviting me to come stay for a weekend. I didn't have transportation, but he graciously volunteered to drive down and pick me up at the apartment Friday after work. It was comforting to spend quality time with the family and to feel a sense of belonging after feeling so alone in the big city.

The whole weekend felt indulgent, a much-needed escape. We went out on a boat, and I got to laugh along with my cousins at the wind whipping our hair around. In the mornings I sat at the kitchen table, talking with my aunt. I loved the way she listened to me and treated me like an adult. Having coffee in the morning with her now felt so grown up. I appreciated having a bed that wasn't on the floor and home-cooked meals instead of the PB&Js I was living on. It was a new experience to hear firsthand from my cousins and learn about their day-to-day lives beyond a couple of sentences of an update in a Christmas card. I spent time playing with and talking to my two small boy cousins who were no longer babies but three and five years old. They were cute, funny, and had sweet voices. I remember when it was time for me to go, the smallest one asked me, "Are you coming back next Sunday (his lisp sounded more like Thunday)?" And I told him probably not, but maybe next summer, and he said, "No, I think you should come back next Sunday." That little weekend trip is time I am so thankful for. I don't know if I ever let him know that, years later, it was something I still appreciated. I don't even know if they remember that visit, but it really made me feel connected to the family. It's something I always think of when I think of my Uncle Steve.

MATERNAL BRANCHES

Our cousin Ryan lived up in the Chicago area when we were growing up. Going to visit him felt like an adventure. He was then and still is just an all-around cool guy. And when I say that, I mean he had the latest stuff to play with, and he did fascinating things—he ice skated, played an instrument, had fun neighborhood friends, and at one point lived in a house with a barn to explore.

One thing he did that I was so jealous of (and I believe my brothers were too) was that he went to the *Bozo the Clown Show* on WGN, and he actually was one of the kids chosen to play the Grand Prize Game. If you got the ping pong ball into bucket #6 in the Grand Prize Game, you won a Schwinn bicycle and a $50 bill (which is close to $200 in 2024!) We could not believe that our cousin actually got to not only meet Bozo but appear on TV and win "swell" prizes, like Monopoly games and clown makeup kits. I don't think Ryan made it past bucket #3, but it is a prime example of some of the cool things he got to do and why we would be envious. We usually saw each other only during the holidays. He played a bit more with my brother Jonathan because they were the same age, but it was always the four of us at the holiday get-togethers sneaking Cokes, playing the nickel slot machine at our great aunt and uncle's house at Christmas time, laughing over presents (the Do-A-Duck build and paint a mallard kit) and during those times, he always felt more like a sibling than a cousin.

When I was in Brazil, he sent me a mixtape that he made —it was new wave music, and it introduced me to several bands, including Depeche Mode. That mixtape sparked a lifelong interest and changed the way that I listened to, heard, felt, and experienced music. When I returned and visited him, he took me to under 21 clubs in Chicago so I could hear the music and dance to the different interpretations by the DJs on each floor. It was loud and vibrant, something he shared that I could not experience in my hometown (remember, this was before Spotify or Apple Music). It was fantastic to be introduced to that scene, and I noticed that wherever we went, people seemed to know who he was, wanting to greet him, almost a little famous. He just let it roll off his back, unaffected. I was proud to be with him and excited to see firsthand something he was passionate about.

His adventures continued after high school with his move to England and the work and life he was exposed to living overseas. I spent a lot of time with him during my visit there in college, meeting his friends, taking photos, and learning from him as he showed me around Windsor. His work there led to future jobs and travel. He is extremely talented in lighting and sound and is a drummer in bands himself. He has traveled around the world, touring with and designing for some of the biggest names in music, but he is still as humble as he was as a teenager and nonchalant about his gifts. We're still impressed, though, Ryan, and will continue to be.

He has generously gotten me and our family into many concerts, and I'm always beyond proud to see his work. He gifted my son with his first concert experience and took him backstage after the show to meet the artist and get a photograph with him to commemorate the impactful moment. It's a lifelong memory that he treasures, especially poignant as he is now interested in the same industry. He also recently shared the backstage experience with my daughter, tour bus, stage, and artist sighting—an unexpected and much-appreciated surprise. I love seeing how he is sharing his musicality and talents with his children, and watching them dance and sing along at his concerts when he's drumming, and seeing videos of him playing guitar and singing with his daughter is a joy. I'm just so thankful for this cousin of mine, who's always felt more like a brother and all that he's given to my life.

MATRIARCH / PATRIARCH

Whomever holds the illustrious title of the Matriarch or Patriarch in a family should be revered. They are the ones who can remember family members past and present farther back than anyone. They are a source of family wisdom like none other. For my birthday in 2013, instead of a birthday gift from my parents, I asked if I could have a trip with my mom to go and visit her aunt, Charlotte. As my grandmother had been gone for ten years at that

point, Aunt Char, as we called her, was the family matriarch at the time, and I wanted to interview her.

My mom went with me because she had some questions, too, so off we flew to Arizona. It was a quick trip,
just a long weekend, but I treasure that time we had. It
was the first time I saw the house that I had been sending Christmas cards and letters to since they retired and
moved south. Aunt Char was my long-time pen pal who
wrote with the most exquisite, precise handwriting on
thick, quality writing paper—the kind that is scrumptious to the touch.

It was also the first time it was just the few of us together, without it being a part of a large family gathering.
We connected in a way that we hadn't before. Over our
morning coffee, sitting around in our jammies and she
in her "housecoat," we shared interviews recorded on a
first-generation iPad. I was able to discover some family
history, much of which my mom was discovering at the
same time, and that triggered more questions from both
of us. I was able to watch Aunt Char as she stared into
the distance, thinking hard to recall family facts that she
hadn't thought about in years.

Some of the details she was able to remember were
fascinating and indicative of older times— ailments of
great-great-grandparents and how they were treated
then. A stroke landed one in the hospital for over a year
because physical therapy wasn't done at the time, but
rather, doctors waited it out to see if the person could
regain the ability to walk. In the end, this particular

great-great-grandmother did not. She was sent home, where she spent the rest of her years in the main living room, then converted by necessity to be her bedroom. I also learned about a relative who had contracted some sort of "crippling arthritis" that was so bad he was unable to walk and got around on a child's tricycle.

I heard her perspective of her relationship with her sister, my grandmother. As the only two siblings, they were close, but there was an undercurrent that could be felt by those around them. This conversation let me hear her story and interpretation, which answered questions that I didn't realize I wanted the answers to before that moment. I learned that in childhood, they were not close, as they were nine years apart. I learned how different my grandmother's childhood was compared to hers. By the time my great-aunt came along, my great-grandfather was sober, which was not true during my grandmother's youth. And that as adults, there was a barrier of resentment my grandmother had toward her, borne from the fact that her family could not afford to send her to college. When it was time for Char to go to college years later, they were much better off financially, and she was able to go to the private school where my parents ended up meeting years later, and even later, my brother and I graduated from.

During a morning conversation, I witnessed Aunt Char's sobering realization at one point that she was it, the last one—she couldn't remember, and there was no one else she could ask questions of. She said how she wished she would have asked her mother some of these facts, stories, and written them down. It reinforced how important it is to preserve these memories, to write down the stories, to share.

Aunt Char did remember that she had something she called her "treasure box." Whenever she wanted to hold on to something but didn't quite know what to do with it, it went in the box. So, we went into the closet, pulled a large hat box down from a high shelf, and explored what was inside: the passage tickets to America, in Swedish, a Swedish Bible from the 1880s, with names and dates written inside, and her wedding album in which her mother had written family tree information, birth dates, full names. It was the only tangible item with that information, and she was able to go back and fill in some blanks of the people she talked about earlier. We spent the afternoon reviewing and marveling with each new discovery we lifted out of that box, saying, "Wow, look at this!" It truly was a treasure box.

I learned some of the history of the generations who came to America from Sweden, the villages our ancestors were from, and how the family name that I always thought was ours wasn't. We were Pearsons, not Holmgrens, as we discovered from some of the documents in that box. Back then names were assumed when a citizen would sponsor an immigrant, a distant Holmgren cousin assuming responsibility for a newly arrived Pearson. We pieced together what we could and lamented over what we could not. She commented, "And there's no one I can ask, doggone it."

So much was learned by all three generations that weekend and during those interviews, I feel so fortunate to have shared that time with her, especially now. My great (and she certainly was Great with a capital G) Aunt Char died on the last day of 2019. Sadly, we were unable to honor her and attend her funeral because the family was waiting until spring to get together when the weather was better, but we all know what happened that spring of 2020. I was not able to say goodbye to her. I do treasure that trip, the time I was able to spend with her, the video I took of her on my iPad (see, I learned to have a digital copy this time). And now my parents are the Matriarch and Patriarch of the two sides of the family. And I'm trying to capture all I can, while I can (doggone it!)

~

REMEMBRANCES

I try to focus on the memories of loved ones, especially those that aren't here, who I miss, rather than that longing and ache in the heart. When I recall some of the things that remind me of them, it brings back moments we shared that provide a warmth and a sense of connection to them (and often a gentle smile). Sometimes, these reminders pop up out of the blue, most often smells or sounds that are familiar, stirring something somewhere in the back of my mind. Lately, I've been trying to be more aware—hoping that actively remembering will prevent me from losing these memories and keep them close.

Some of these remembrances I'm including here. Maybe you have similar ones of your loved ones that bring you comfort and make you smile...

I remember my Poppa's giggle and the smell of his pipe. Taking me with him when he ran errands, often treating me to a Charleston Chew, which I never could find in our town, was a special treat. Whenever I enjoy one, I think of him and riding in his car, the smell of the leather seats, the pipe resting on the center console, and the sweetness of the chocolate.

I remember my Grandma giving raspberry kisses, tickling my cheeks. How she tagged along every visit to watch every basketball, soccer, tennis, and baseball game. I recall her love for baking sweets of all kinds, but pies (strawberry rhubarb and apple) and cookies, especially. She reminded us to count our blessings and was never without Doublemint gum and a Kleenex under her watch band, and she'd share both if you asked.

I remember my Grandmommy's avid love of reading and devotion to her morning crossword puzzle, watching Jeopardy (which I do daily and think of her), listening to Frank Sinatra, referred to by her as "my Frankie," and how privileged I felt to chat with her and watch as she "put on her face" using the little double-sided magnifying mirror, or while I sat at her perfectly set table, feeling like an esteemed guest.

I remember my Nana smelling like Noxzema (she had the softest skin), her babushkas, how she loved the Cubs, walked every day for exercise, the watermelon-y scent of her Max Factor lipstick, and how she didn't say brush your teeth but "wash your teeth."

I remember holding my baby cousin Allison and giving her a bottle when she was about six or seven months old and how deeply she looked into my eyes. If I made a face, she laughed in response. It was such a sweet little moment of connection with this beautiful baby girl, and I was endeared to her from that moment on.

When I remember these things, it makes me smile. And oh, the hugs from them...so enveloping and safe, making you feel so loved, connected, such a part of family.

~

REFLECT AND CONNECT

When you think about your extended family, your whole, big, beautiful, expanded tree:

- Is there someone whose impact on your life immediately comes to mind?
- What qualities of theirs do you see in yourself (that you are grateful for)?
- What are some of the traditions you had growing up with extended family? What was your favorite? Are there any that your family continues?
- Who was always the best joketeller at family gatherings?
- Did anyone ever give you something that you cherish and still have?

- Are there family members you don't get to see often but wish you did? What can you share with them that would feel like a meaningful connection?
- Are there any family members whose military service you want to honor by learning more about or acknowledging them, sharing gratitude for their service?
- For those who are no longer here, consider reaching out and sharing a memory of a loved one whom you miss and what it is you miss about them with someone else who knew them. This might be an object, activity, or product that makes you think of them whenever you see, hear, or smell it, or maybe a phrase they often said or were known for.
- Find out if they remember similar things, and maybe they will share something completely new with you.

I hope when you remember and share these memories that they make you smile too.

CHAPTER 6

GRATEFUL FOR FAITH

*"Faith shows the reality of what we hope for; it is the
evidence of things we cannot see."*
—Hebrews 11:1, NLT

When we were young kids, we didn't have a home church. Our family was faith mutts—I had one grandparent who was Catholic, one who was Lutheran, one who was Methodist, and one who I never knew, but I would guess that he was likely atheist. On my mother's side, there is also some Jewish heritage from a few generations back. I remember often spending the night with my friend and going with her to the Presbyterian church. I loved Sunday school and was jealous I wasn't part of that.

Catechism classes on Wednesday nights seemed like THE social gathering—another place that I seemed to be missing out on, especially after hearing about it the next day at school. And the Vacation Bible Schools at the churches were full of activities and sounded like one more thing I was missing out on until I was luckily invited along one year by a friend. I learned and sang songs that I hadn't heard before that everyone else seemed to know. There were arts and crafts and playing games out-side, breaking up into small groups. There were stories like Jonah being swallowed by the whale and about Job (whose name I always thought they mispronounced) that were new to me. I wanted to have a church home, too, and when I came home and asked my mom about it, she said they hadn't yet found a place that felt like theirs yet. We did a lot of church shopping. After attending most of them, I knew what the insides of most of the churches in my town looked like and who went to each, but none of them felt like I belonged there.

REVEREND FRED

When I was in middle school, we did start regularly at-tending one, the Congregational Church. It was a small congregation, maybe 100-150 people a week, mostly old-er folks who had been attending for years. The church was an old, simple brick building without air conditioning or elaborate stained-glass windows or a bunch of young people like my friends' churches had. But this church, built in the 1850s, had charming French blue walls with a grand white organ with gold accents as the centerpiece of the sanctuary. The crimson carpeting was a stark con-trast and gave the room a sense of crispness. The tall, thick-paned, distorted glass windows invited the light in, which gave it an airy and expansive feel.

Being an old church, the pervasive scent was musty, and, in the summertime, that was mixed with a distinct aroma of damp wood. I remember that smell of the church and the after-church fellowship time. My brothers and I did not look forward to the obligatory hand-shaking and fellowship as we were anxious to head home. But we didn't put up much of a fuss for two reasons: one was the hope for cookies or some other sweet treat being offered in the Joy Prairie Parlor while the grown-ups had coffee, and the other was that it would prolong getting in the car and potentially Dad would forget that my brother had taped KICK ME notes on some unsuspecting, but sweet older congregants who unluckily sat in the pew in front of us and didn't notice they were walking around with it, on their back of their sport coat or the butt of their skirt. It might prolong the telling-off.

I remember how awkward it was when they had the kids' sermon/story time and called us up front because I wasn't really a young child. There were only a handful of kids, so you felt like all the eyes were on you. And then, when the kids were dismissed, I felt unsure about where to go when the kids headed back to the nursery. I often went with the kids just to not have to go back and sit down and listen to the sermon and the songs. I'd have rather helped babysit the younger kids. Overall, I felt completely out of place. It was not a comfort, it was not a joy, we were forced to attend. It was nothing like my friends' churches—singing the old-fashioned hymns, hardly any people my own age, getting dressed up in itchy and uncomfortable clothes. Things changed when we got a new pastor, Fred.

Fred had wild, curly hair, a booming laugh, and told great stories. His telling of the Bible stories was actually compelling and entertaining. He connected to the young folks in a way that I didn't know was possible, and he listened to us, made us feel important. Soon after he started at our church, he launched a confirmation class, and I was one of the five people my age in the church whose parents signed them up to attend. People I normally would not hang out with, wouldn't say hi to in school, and didn't run in the same social circles with, so it was awkward. We were all there for the same reason: because we were forced by our parents. The first few minutes of that first class were dominated by surly or disinterested looks from us, the unwilling participants.

Class met in his office; my parents dropped me off for the hour-long session, and we sat in chairs in a circle amidst the books and piles. I could have kept myself busy just looking around at all of the many books, but Fred was engaging. He talked about things and told us stories in a way that we could relate to. He drew us in and talked with us rather than at us. He shared that the Bible was made of stories to teach us how to live, how to love each other, and Jesus. He openly discussed things we found hard to believe without judging us or questioning our thoughts, ideas, or feelings. We had conversations about what these stories meant, how we saw connections to them in our lives. It was a whole different experience, one of awe and wonder, something I was not used to feeling in church, especially my church.

He arranged activities so we could do things as a group and get to know each other outside of that cluttered and stuffy church office. And while this is commonplace today, it wasn't in the late 1970s/early 1980s, at least not in my town. We went to see the St. Louis Cardinals at Busch Stadium, and he whooped louder than we did, eating a hot dog with gusto. It was the first time a pastor seemed human, real, interesting, and it made me want to listen even more to what he had to say.

The most memorable thing he did was take us on a road trip to the closest synagogue, 30 miles away, to witness a Bar Mitzvah ceremony. It was fascinating to watch the sacred traditions of the ceremony from the balcony, how the young man was supported by family, how they participated with him and the rabbi, and how the congregation all celebrated and looked upon him with pride and acceptance. It was astonishing to see how they came together, in the familiarity of the ritual, knowing what came next, how they commemorated the young man, Ben. And we were amazed at how he could remember everything, how he knew what to do next, and how to read the Hebrew scroll. I don't think I looked away for one second, it was mesmerizing. After the service, Fred took us down to the front and introduced us to the rabbi. They seemed familiar and friendly with each other. I didn't know what to do, to shake his hand or bow or what. I'm pretty sure I stood frozen, taking it all in, but I remember feeling honored to be there.

We did not stay for the celebration party after, so we did not get to see the glass smashing, but Fred told us about that after we piled back into the van and headed home. He asked us what we thought about it and it was interesting to all share our impressions. He reminded us that Jesus was Jewish. He wanted us to see different interpretations, and he wanted to expose us to new perspectives.

I never knew what happened to Reverend Fred. I overheard my mom saying she was sure he was snapped up by a bigger church somewhere because he was just that good, and he likely was. It was the first time I felt that faith made sense, that it was for everyone, not just special people who attended a specific church and performed specific rites. I felt connected for the first time and fascinated and yearned to know more. That was Fred's gift to me (and probably all five of us in the class that year). Thank you, Rev. Fred, wherever you are, for this change in perspective, for igniting an interest and making me feel like faith was accessible and meant for everyone.

~

"Faith is deliberate confidence in the character of God whose ways you may not understand at the time." —Oswald Chambers[14]

I'm going to break my guideline of talking about childhood here because I had two times, more recently, that I am so grateful for. I can't reflect on the theme of faith without mentioning them.

---

[14] Chambers, Oswald. *My Utmost for His Highest*. Barbour Publishing, 1935. Original quote reads: "Faith is not intelligent understanding, faith is deliberate commitment to a Person where I see no way."

PASTOR KELLY

At my lowest low, I felt completely lost and stuck because I knew in my heart of hearts that I shouldn't stay in my marriage. It had gotten to the point of being detrimental to me and my health and therefore, I couldn't be the best mother and support for my children. However, I was staying in the marriage because I thought it was what God wanted me to do. I didn't want to break my marriage vows; I took them seriously and I struggled and delayed making a decision that I didn't want to make because I was worried that God would be mad at me.

By chance, a friend who I hadn't seen in a while met me for lunch during this low time. After we had our food and were seated, she looked at me and asked how I was. Instead of the usual automatic response, "I'm good, all's fine," with a pasted-on smile that I had been giving everyone who asked this question for many months, I looked at her and just let it all spill out. I don't know what made me be honest with her in that moment, on that day, but I did not hold back and told her exactly how awful I was feeling and some of the things that were going on. She looked at me with empathy in her caring eyes and said that she thought that I knew what I needed to do, so she wanted to know what it was that was holding me back.

I knew she was a person who understood faith, and so I was honest again and told her I was worried about God. That He would be mad at me, that He didn't want me to do this, that it was going against His will.

She asked if I had talked to a pastor about it, and I told her I had not because I didn't want to talk to the pastors at my church and then show up there with my family on Sundays. It felt too personal to talk about with anyone I saw regularly. Plus, I had never met the pastors, just waved or smiled in passing, so I didn't feel close to them. I explained to her that it felt hypocritical to attend as if nothing was wrong after sharing this. I was afraid. And in saying this to her, I felt a weight had been lifted after admitting how I was feeling. In voicing it, though, it was now out there; it was real.

She was quiet in thought for a moment and then said she knew someone I could talk with if I would be willing to. She knew they could listen with understanding about my situation and help me explore and navigate through some of the questions I had. She said she thought my talking to her would be helpful and that I didn't have to make any decisions, just talk, so I agreed. Within 24 hours, she had contacted this pastor, the wife of someone she worked with, and told her about me. She let me know that the pastor would indeed be willing to meet with me and shared her contact information. I sent her an email with my heart racing, nervous by what I had set in motion.

Pastor Kelly reached out to me almost immediately. I didn't realize at the time she was not only working as a pastor, but was also a mother to an infant. Even so, she worked it out so that she could meet me during the workday over my lunch hour. We ended up meeting at a restaurant off the highway, halfway between my location and hers, and had lunch together. She had her new baby in the car carrier with her and she listened to what I was struggling with, my questions, doubts, and fears, and she comforted me. She suggested some resources that helped me to see the situation through a different lens and provided insight that was much more valuable than months of therapy visits had been.

She said, "God doesn't want you to be unhappy and in a situation that is not healthy for you." I had not thought about it like that before. She helped me feel comfortable enough to speak from my heart, and it was such a relief to do so after hiding my feelings for so many months. The perspective she gave me about the questions and doubts I was struggling with was life-altering in that it helped me to see my situation more clearly, and it made me feel that a path forward was possible and that I could find the support to navigate next steps.

I don't know where Pastor Kelly is now, but I'm so grateful for this conversation. I was broken, nervous about being judged, so worried about God being upset with me that I was paralyzed into inaction because of it. My head was swirling and panicked, and shallow breathing and sleepless nights had become my norm, but after talking and praying with her that day, for the first time in a few years, I had a small sense that everything was going to be ok.

I'm grateful that my friend was thoughtful enough to put me in touch with someone she knew could help and that a pastor went out of her way to meet with me and help provide peace to a hurting soul.

~

"Faith consists in believing when it is beyond the power of reason to believe." — *Voltaire*[15]

PASTOR CHRIS

After I had made the decision to proceed with a divorce, we continued to live together for a while, which was awkward, but we felt it was best for the kids. I still loved him and cared for his well-being. I hoped that we could work together to make the transition as easy as possible and to support each other as best we could. Unfortunately, that is not how everything played out, but that was my hope and intention. One of the things that he had asked me to do was to go and talk with the pastor he had been meeting with at our church. At the time, I thought that the pastor would talk me out of it, and that's why he wanted me to go so badly. I was reluctant and thought he would negatively judge me for seeking a divorce. I felt embarrassed to speak with someone from our church, and I also felt almost like there was an ulterior motive for him suggesting I go, but I agreed, and I am so glad I did.

Instead of judgment or pressure, what I found in Pastor Chris was just an amazing listener. He's empathetic,

---

[15] https://quotefancy.com/quote/759663/Voltaire-Faith-consists-in-believing-when-it-is-beyond-the-power-of-reason-to-believe

reasonable, and supportive on so many levels. I believe that he was placed in my life for a reason, as most people are when we look in hindsight. When I went to meet with him for the first time, I was confused and still very much afraid that God was going to be mad at me for seeking a divorce. I was struggling a lot with my faith and not wanting to break my marriage vows, and I felt tremendous guilt about what it would do to my family, to my kids especially. I desperately wanted to protect them.

He was such an easy person to talk to, to pray with, and he continued to counsel and support both of us for many months—through the divorce and beyond. He was there for our family. He made sure that we both felt comfortable continuing to attend church there and that the kids felt connected with the student pastors and their group leaders. Both of them decided to be baptized and that was because we felt comfortable and a continued connection, which I don't think we would've had if it wouldn't have been for Pastor Chris being welcoming and looking out for us.

I don't know how my family could have gotten through that time without him and his wisdom, guidance, and prayers. He even helped mediate upon occasion, which I know could not have been comfortable for him, but he prioritized being there to support us over his comfort.

At the time, he was the Group Life Pastor, and he suggested a small group that he thought would be beneficial for me to join. That group itself was such a gift—the ladies from that group are my girls; they've become close friends and a source of comfort. We get together regularly, and I met them all thanks to Pastor Chris.

Over those months, he provided me with Scripture to ponder and reflect on, and the message he kept reiterating was that he wanted me to know that God still loves me. I think that was the thing that was holding me back from making that terribly tough decision.

I look in amazement at the timing; both Kelly and Chris entered my life at a time when I was lost, anxious, fearful. Their presence and their counsel helped move me from being stuck. God really does put people in our lives for a reason, leading us to our purpose and leading us to comfort. I am so thankful for them both and for the realization to be open to the people He places in your life, for we never know when they might change our path. It's very likely I would not be focused on gratitude and writing this book had I not experienced these encounters. But I am grateful, and I know no matter what, God is with me.

~

REFLECT AND CONNECT

In thinking back over some challenges you've had in life and how faith played a role...

- Do you remember a time when you thought your situation was unsurmountable—who was placed in your life that helped you through it?

- What signs or feelings let you know that God was present?
- When and how have you been curious about other faiths, and what did you learn about your own through this new perspective?
- When was a time you felt led to do something not because of logic but that you just felt called to do? How did that turn out? What are you grateful for from that experience?
- What verses were shared with you that you leaned on during a tough time, and who shared them with you?
- What is a time you realized that someone was placed in your life for a reason? Did you see it at the time?
- Reach out to those who shared these moments with you, and let them know how they impacted you or your circumstances. If you are unable to reach them personally, a prayer of gratitude is a beautiful way of showing your thanks.

CHAPTER 7

GRATEFUL FOR FRIENDSHIP

"There is nothing I would not do for those who are really my friends. I have no notion of loving people by halves, it is not my nature." — *Jane Austen*[16]

Friendship takes many forms. From our earliest memories of playing with neighborhood kids and classmates, learning to share, to take turns, to give an "I'm sorry" hug when there are tears over spilled finger paints or pinched fingers. As we grow, they are there with us when we experience our first crush. We watch after-school specials with them and learn about and experiment the latest trends with them. We broaden our circle with new friends as we take on new interests, join teams, clubs. And during those challenging teenage years, they are alongside us as we learn some lessons the hard way (didn't we see this in an after-school special?) and then commiserate together through the consequences of those lessons. We are influenced by them, and we try on different personas as we learn who we are. Often, our

---

[16] Austen, Jane. *Northanger Abbey*. 1818.

friends see something in us that we don't, thereby reflecting back to us some of our unique gifts and qualities.

~

"Make new friends, but keep the old, one is silver and the other gold."[17] —Girl Scout song

GOLD FRIENDS

When I think of my gold friends, Steven immediately comes to mind. I've known him at least since high school, although it's likely longer. My mom tells me we were little buddies in Mighty Mights swim class at the YMCA when we were toddlers. If that's true, it means my younger self instinctively knew what a gem he was and gravitated toward him before I had the capacity to make logical decisions.

Steven and I became reacquainted in high school my sophomore year over shamrock shakes on a Mickey D's run during South Pacific play practice. But we became close friends after I returned from Brazil and was having a hard time fitting back into the social structure of small town high school after such a life-changing year. I remember being excited to share my experiences with some of my BB (before Brazil) friends and they dropped by to "check me out" after I came back, unannounced, so I wasn't expecting them. I had gained weight in Brazil, which I blame on the food, but really it was from my

---

[17] *Making New Friends Song*. Girl Scouts of the USA, https://my.girlscouts.org/content/dam/girlscouts-vtk/local/aid/meetings/D14DP04/Making-New-Friends-Song.pdf. Accessed 4 Sept. 2024.

jumping in with gusto to all I encountered, wanting to taste and experience everything I came across. And what I found that I liked, I could not control myself with, especially the cheese bread (pão de queijo) and the chocolates.

They came down to my basement room, and because I hadn't seen them for a year, I was excited to show them some things I had brought back: my Brazilian flag, photos of friends and family, and my dangling stone earrings. I wanted to tell them about my year. I'd just had this incredible experience, and I wanted to share some of the highlights with them. They didn't seem interested in any stories or in actually looking at the pictures. From their disapproving looks and sideways glances at each other, I felt they couldn't get past how I had ballooned up. I felt a sense of dread, a sinking in the pit of my stomach as I realized we were not the same anymore. This was my first indication that my senior year was going to be a completely different high school experience.

But there was a group who turned out to be interested in hearing about my year—my new gang; I just didn't know they were my new gang yet. The leader of the gang was Steven, akin to Anthony Michael Hall's character in Sixteen Candles, who was the self-proclaimed King of the Dipshits. He had (and has) an innate leadership quality that draws in those around him, ever creative and exciting. He has a way of making you feel like anything is possible, that no dream is unrealistic, and that anything can be an adventure just waiting to be experienced. And while he was definitely the leader of this gang, he transcended the stifling boundaries of cliques in the 80s high school, as he was one of the rare few that could connect and befriend and be accepted by anyone: jock, Future Farmer of America, kid who camped out in The Pit (in-school suspension), popular girl. He was a little magical in that way.

Everything was fun when Steven was around—he was always cooking up some sort of escapade. He was the director, leading the group of friends in making home movies. One of these was a repeated series called "The Ask Professor Harvey Wallbanger Show," where the main character Harvey (aka Tim) interviewed such "celebrities" as Todd, doing his best impression of Dr. Ruth Westheimer or the other Todd appearing with a solemn bow as his mysterious character, Master Po. Or when he'd take you through the Hardees drive-through, which was THE place to hang out and order 20 big cookies, and the cashier would say, "Sorry sir, we don't have 20 right now. We have 12." Without hesitation, he announced into the drive-through speaker, "Ok, then I'll take 12!" Giggles erupted from all the passengers in the back seat of the 1977 International Scout with the baby doll strapped to the front grill who were along for the ride that day. And there was never a shortage of people wanting to go along for the ride. You never knew what you were in for when you were going to hang out with Steven; you just knew it was going to be fun, and you wouldn't feel confined to the small midwestern town and its ways, but instead, like doors you never noticed before were opening, inviting you to walk through and look around.

Because Steven was more focused on adventures than schoolwork, he often left school and was a frequent resident of The Pit. One of my defining life moments happened during my senior year when I was in the middle of giving a speech in my English class. I hated public speaking (still do) and had felt like I never quite fit in or like I belonged after I returned from Brazil. To add to this sense of feeling like an outsider, I was also the only senior in the junior English class, as that class was a requirement for graduation. My speech was about Marilyn Monroe, one of my obsessions during high school, and what I recall was suddenly feeling hot and woozy and having tunnel vision. The next thing I remember was feeling exhausted, thinking I was in bed and my dad was shaking me awake, "Jennifer, Jennifer." When I opened my eyes, I discovered it wasn't my dad; it was my English teacher, Mr. Kennedy, and I was lying face-down on the floor. The class was silent and stunned; wide eyes and open-mouthed faces were staring at me.

What actually happened, as I pieced together later from accounts of horrified classmates who were all too happy to share details, was that I leaned forward and said, very dramatically (one even said I did it with a Marilyn voice), "I think I'm going to faint." Then I fell backward, stiff like a tree, bounced against the projector, which came crashing down as I then fell forward. After I came to, I think I said, "I want to go home." Someone helped me up and escorted me to the nurse's office. I don't remember who. What I do remember is them asking who I would like to call and knowing my parents were both working and not home. Knowing that Steven wasn't at school that day, I asked the nurse to call him. Of course, he was at home and willing to come to my rescue. He took me to his house and made up a bed on the couch for me to rest. And yes, I was horrified for the rest of the year in English class and chose to take the gift of a "C" rather than attempt another shot at the speech. But to this day, I remember who came to my aid in a moment of not only weakness but mortification, and that was my good pal Steven. He was there for me in high school and has been there for me ever since, always supporting me— sometimes by listening, sometimes by pepping me up, sometimes through gifts and experiences.

One example was when my cat, Kricktstein, died during college. Steven was the one I called when I couldn't stop crying. He had lost a beloved cat a few years earlier and could relate to the loss I was feeling. My crying was so uncontrollable the day after Krickey died that I was not even able to speak during a class presentation. My partner for the assignment had to do it—thank you, Andy! After class, Steven showed up at my dorm with a Spiegel's box, and out popped a little black kitty he had bought for me to help ease my grief. He said it was a girl, so I named her Cleopatra. At the first visit to the vet, I found out the fluffball had been misgendered and Cleopatra became Cleopatrick. I successfully hid Cleo from my resident director for about a week before the meowing gave us away, and I had to take him to live at my parents' house, but what a comforting surprise.

After college, when I was unemployed, Steven came through again, helping me land my first "real" job at a local radio station where he worked. I covered the afternoon news stories, making daily rounds to the courthouse and police station to report the court beat and anything else noteworthy that had happened that day on the 5:00 news. I covered the county fair activities, Little Miss Princess and Miss Morgan County, the stock car races, the talent shows, the 4-H Winners, and any "big stories" that happened in a small town, like when the governor showed up or college graduation events; it was an interesting first job. One of the things I remember most from that radio job, though, was an assignment Steven brought me along on.

His job at the station was both copywriter and host of a couple of entertainment-focused shows. Because of his entertainment focus, he was asked to keep a visiting entertainer, well, entertained for the day. That visitor happened to be Dweezil Zappa, who was in town to promote guitars at a local music shop. It made sense that Steven was the one tasked with this, as he was the same age as Dweezil and the most likely to provide a fun (or the least embarrassing small-town) day for him. There wasn't much to do in our town, so Steven gathered up the entourage and took everyone swimming at the Country Club. They were staying at the nicest hotel in our town at the time, the Holiday Inn. That evening, we hung out there with them and played a part in some trick that apparently was repeated in every city they visited. We were asked to knock on one of the band member's doors with a birthday cake with lit candles and to break into song, (Happy Birthday, of course) when he opened the door. My recollection of that day is that it felt surreal, hanging out with a band. But Steven was leading us all and I was again struck by how he could get along with everyone, finding a common ground, bringing a level of comfort to all he encountered.

In the 90s, he invited me out to Los Angeles to visit him when I was going through a rough patch in a relationship. It was already a refreshing change of pace to get away for a few days in the sunshine and spend some time with him and his family. He had another surprise for me when I arrived. He took me as his guest to a taping of the show Friends. It was the episode "The One That Could Have Been" where their lives are alternate reality: Phoebe was the stockbroker, Ross was still married to Carol, Monica hadn't lost the weight, Joey hooked up with Rachel who was married to Barry, and Chandler was a struggling writer and Joey's PA. Remember that one? Sitting in the front row of the studio audience watching the process, seeing the retakes up close, was an amazing experience with a cherished friend. It's a memory I'm even more thankful for having experienced due to the recent passing of Matthew Perry. I'm so grateful to have the memory of that day with Steven, watching the Friends in action in the studio, feeling the energy of the audience.

His support has spanned decades: he was there for me during my divorce and job changes, and he checks in regularly to see how my family and I are doing. He always remembers to ask specifically about my dad and his health. This is especially sweet, as the first time my dad met him, he was a bit dubious of Steven, who walked into our house sporting the red leather Michael Jackson jacket complete with white glove. Not kidding. Although we live across the country now and we don't get to see each other often, when we do, it's as if no time has passed. I know that he is always just a phone call away, and I sincerely hope that I have reciprocated some of the encouragement he has given me through the years.

Steven is a creative—a designer and screenwriter, and has often commented that we should collaborate on a writing project someday. I aspire to write together at some point, but what's held me back so far is the worry that he thinks I'm better than I am, that he will cheer on even bad ideas because that's who he is—he rallies for you, he's there for you, and makes you believe you can do anything. I am thankful for his championing support and for the experiences he introduced in my life.

I found out that the Mighty Mights program still exists at some YMCAs—it's marketed as "sports fun for toddlers." May two other toddlers be so lucky as to form a friendship like ours.

⁓

I'm embarrassed to share how I chose my college because it was not the most sound reasoning—something along the lines of a crush on a professional tennis player that I knew lived nearby whom I was determined to meet. But however I ended up there, I believe it was meant to be because that year, my freshman year in Michigan, I met a lifelong friend, my roommate, Lila.

Lila was like no one I had ever met. She was small but took up space with her vivacious energy and her raucous and highly contagious laugh. She had vibrant red hair, made deeper by henna, which I had not heard of before. She was also from a small town but was less sheltered than me—she was a year older but much more life-experienced and independent, and she really took me under her wing. She was another one who never met someone she could not befriend. She had friends from every single college clique: the black leather jacket-Patchouli-wearing goth types, nerdy philosophy majors, cocky-jock football players, country music-loving and mullet-sporting small town guys, first-generation college students from the heart of Detroit and snooty sorority sisters. She had friends everywhere and introduced me to them all.

She drove a little maroon Honda stick shift like a maniac and would let me join her on trips to the mall or to grab a pack of Newport Lights or our favorite treats, Screaming Yellow Zonkers and Cape Cod potato chips. Because I was far from home (over an eight-hour drive), she invited me to her home for Easter, and I was welcomed by her sweet parents, who even had a filled basket for me on Easter morning. By then, she was certainly starting to feel like family.

We would jump up and down on the beds blasting "Push It" by Salt-n-Pepa and run pencils or the handles of hairbrushes along the radiator to annoy the guys who lived below us. They were jerks toward us because they thought we were weirdos, so we played along to their stereotype, obnoxiously getting even in our own weird way.

Lila acquainted me with many firsts by letting me participate and experience alongside her. She took me to various parties around campus and to my first underground club in Detroit. I didn't drink back then but didn't feel a desire to—I could easily become intoxicated just with the people-watching. She also invited me on an overnight visit to a classmate's home, which proved an eye-opening experience on many levels as their family was likely living in poverty. It was a pivotal weekend for me. I realized how truly lucky I was, and many of the things I had taken for granted my whole life I sharply became grateful for: heat, water, parents with jobs. I had a lot more empathy and admiration for our classmate, who also was very social, could get along with anyone, and who laughed a lot. I realized she had more to work for than me and our other classmates. I appreciated Lila for knowing how she lived and not making a big deal out of it or treating her any differently and for allowing me to see it too.

While Lila is bold, lively, and has a social presence, she was then and still is very calming and maternal in nature. I remember being really sick, and it was the first time being so far away from home. Lila took care of me and actually found me collapsed on the hallway floor on the way to the bathroom. She picked me up and helped me down to the bathroom and back again and made sure I had what I needed to feel better. Once, I was frustrated with my hair and had the brilliant idea of cutting my own bangs. When she arrived back in the room and saw the mess I'd made of my hair, she first had a good laugh, and then she took me right to Regis in the mall to find a stylist who could repair the damage as best as they could. Then, she took me to experience my first gyro on the way back to our dorm.

She modeled self-sufficiency. She worked in the evenings after going to classes during the day. This provided her with a life outside of school, even more broad contacts, like an off-campus boyfriend, and spending money. I admired and looked up to her (and still do).

I left after freshman year, and we kept in touch sporadically. The day I got married, I received a call, and when my mom handed me the phone with a quizzical look, signaling she didn't know who was calling, I heard, "Guess who this is?" and I knew right away. When I said, "Lila!" I was met with that familiar one-of-a-kind laugh. What a great way to start the day!

After going so many years without regularly being in my life, we reconnected serendipitously in the late '90s when I moved back to Michigan. I was overjoyed to discover she was living in the city where I worked. She was now married, and she and her husband quickly became family, yet again, and remain so today. As an adult friend, she has continued to be a source of such support throughout the year—my concert-going buddy, godmother to my daughter, wise counsel, and confidante. Her farm has been my respite during troubled times, and just her presence and welcoming arms have given me the light I needed on dark days.

She can still talk and befriend anyone and has a way about her that instinctively takes care of people, nourishing their bodies and spirits with her amazing cooking, hospitality, caring nature, love, and laughter, oh, the Lila laughter.

BRAVE FRIENDS

Our friends laugh and love with us; they boost us through struggles, and sometimes that boost comes through bravery—their bravery to confront us with a hard truth that can change the path we are on, leading us back to where we should be.

There have been a couple of friends who have confronted me over the last decade with some pretty hard truths, ones I definitely didn't want to hear and, at the time, dismissed. But in their eyes, I saw kindheartedness. That allowed me to forgo my usual retort of excuses, as you do when you don't want to admit something, and instead, I listened to what they had to say.

After months and years of pretending everything was ok in my marriage, downplaying scenarios, and avoiding topics where it might be raised, I was having dinner with a friend and let some comments during a recent interaction between him and me slip out. I immediately tried to cover and backtrack because of the shame and embarrassment I felt at letting someone speak to me that way. But it was too late; I could see her eyes widen, and she said, "Jenn, that's not right." Again, I tried to downplay it, but the more questions she asked, the more honest I became. She was asking with a tone of love and feelings of concern, and at that moment, I felt safe enough to open up and share. And so, a few more examples came out. And at the end, she didn't judge, which is what I think I was most afraid of. But instead, she simply asked me what I would say to her if she were telling me the same stories.

I felt my heart sink as those words snapped me into a realization that I hadn't been ready to face. Because what I would have told her would have been exactly what I didn't want to hear but needed to. And her honesty and bravery to tell me what I didn't want to hear started a shift that set me on a new, very difficult, but better path.

She continued to be supportive when we were able to get together in the years that followed, but I still look back at that initial confrontation that truly caused a shift with such gratitude. And also to my work friends, who then helped support me through the day-to-day of the following few years. You know who you are, but I don't know if you know how much it truly meant to me. Your daily check-ins, rallying, sound advice, sympathetic ears, always willing to listen without judgment, making me smile or laugh when it got too heavy. I could not have survived those years without you, and I thank you with my whole heart.

"No friendship is an accident." — O. Henry[18]

REFLECT AND CONNECT

It's your turn to think about the friendships you've had through the years, especially the long-lasting ones with those who have seen you through many phases of your life.

- What's your earliest memory of something you did together?
- What are some of the things you remember regularly doing when you were younger that you still do together?
- Do you have any "traditions" with your friends you look forward to and that you feel define your friendship?
- When was a friend brave enough to tell you the truth when others wouldn't?
- Or when did they challenge you, change your perspective or set you on a new path?
- When was a time that a friend made you feel completely loved and supported? (Have you told them how they made you feel?)
- What is your best adventure together or the wildest thing you've done with a friend? Did it change your friendship?

---

[18] O. Henry. *Heart of the West.* Doubleday, Page & Company, 1907.

- What is your sweetest memory with a friend, the one that always warms your heart when you think about it?

Reach out and share an old photo or a song from that time, let them know you remember and are grateful for the experience, maybe add a little adult perspective after reflecting. You just might receive some remembrances of theirs in return that brighten your day.

CHAPTER 8

GRATEFUL FOR ADVENTURE

"Life is short, make every day an adventure."
—Unknown[19]

Adventures can happen in everyday life, anytime an experience evokes awe and wonder. For me, travel provides the perfect atmosphere for an adventure. Some of these adventures I had while traveling in Brazil included experiencing Carnaval, the entire country celebrating the kickoff to Lent and experiencing the World Cup. But it was a trip to England a few years after returning from Brazil that I will never forget, one that turned out differently than expected.

～

ADVENTURES WITH LIFELONG IMPACT

My aunt was a flight attendant for PanAm, based in London, and lived right outside the city of Windsor, England. For my Christmas present that year, she invited me to come spend the holiday break with her in London. It just

---

[19] https://www.mymountainsandme.com/blog/adventure-quotes

so happened that my college had something called January term (J-term), which was an intensive where you took one class only and covered a semester's worth of content during that month. The Spring semester didn't start until February. Two of these J-terms were required to graduate, but for the other two years, you got a really long Christmas break. So, I planned to skip this J-term to spend even longer with my aunt and cousin in London, a full six weeks. One of the weeks, we arranged for her to companion-fly me to Germany to stay with a friend who was a foreign exchange student living in Hamburg.

The trip started with a huge surprise when, at the Detroit airport, she revealed she'd upgraded us to fly First Class for the international flight. I could not believe the luxurious seat, the ridiculously scrumptious prime rib on actual plates with linen napkins. I loved my little navy leather PanAm bag of toiletries and used it for decades after that trip. She knew most of the crew and was even able to take me into the cockpit for an introduction to the pilot and co-pilot while in flight. I had no idea how soon that practice was going to change.

It was awesome to reconnect with my cousin, who I hadn't seen for a couple of years since he and my aunt had moved to England. He was working on the lighting crew at the Windsor Ballet, and when he was not working and my aunt was away, we explored together— taking moody black-and-white photos of us on the Long Walk, drinking warm Cokes in his favorite restaurant, visiting his friends and the shops on the High Street and eating Toblerone. He taught me you could tell an American by their shoes, and he was with me when I bought a pair of black brogues with GB on them so I could better fit in. I was amazed at how comfortable he was living abroad, how completely acclimated both he and my aunt were with their new life, their new routine.

When my aunt was not working (on a flight), we had our own adventures. She rented a car, and we drove up to Oxford and Stratford-upon-Avon. It was the first time she had driven on the wrong side of the road with a left-handed stick shift, and there were several instances of running up over the curb on those windy, cobblestone streets, especially in the narrow streets of Oxford. There were a lot of "watch out!" and fits of laughter. But oh, how we took in the vistas of the countryside—the rolling green hills with the sheep grazing everywhere we looked amidst the morning mist. We had the new Pet Shop Boys cassette and listened to that on repeat up and down the motorways, through the villages, singing more loudly each time we heard a song and became familiar with the lyrics (you couldn't just pull them up on Apple Music then—you had to memorize them, which I'm sure my kids find hard to believe.)

I went to my first Hard Rock Cafe and spent more money than I should have on a sweatshirt—it was not just the regular Hard Rock one, though. It was a special edition Christmas 1988 version, and I HAD to have it. We saw a lot that day, up London—the steps of St. Paul's Cathedral where the bird lady in Mary Poppins sang "Feed the Birds," and we watched the street entertainers. However, the tone of the trip changed after we arrived back in the flat in Windsor from the train we had boarded that afternoon at Victoria Station.

My aunt's answering machine was blinking with multiple messages, the first one a frantic message in French from a friend, a fellow flight attendant. She called her back before listening to the rest, and that is when we learned about PanAm flight 103. The Clipper Maid of the Seas had exploded that day over Lockerbie, Scotland, with several of my aunt's coworkers and friends onboard. The remainder of the messages were from friends and family wanting to make sure she had not been on the flight, as she was originally scheduled to be on it. She often shared her monthly schedule with family in case she was in the States or anywhere near them to meet up, so the messages were frantic. She quickly called them back, and we were glued to the news.

The next few weeks were blanketed with fear, disbelief, and sadness over the unthinkable tragedy. As more information surfaced and more stories of her colleagues who had been on the flight became known, I became aware of how much more personal this was for her. She began having nightmares of falling where she would jolt awake in the bed next to me. I was afraid for her to fly again. She comforted me by telling me that she was not afraid because everyone was on high alert and they were checking more carefully than ever before. I saw this myself when I left England to return home, and the level of security was so different than it had been on my trip over. Gone was the lightness and excitement of frivolous travelers off to new places. The atmosphere was somber and scary, with guards everywhere, extra security checks, and stickers on bags for each of the multiple checkpoints, now requiring you to arrive three or four hours prior to the flight instead of the normal two. It had suddenly become a new travel era.

That trip had a profound impact on me. It was unsettling to be there at such a time and so close to someone directly affected. I was thankful at the time for the whole experience, for what my aunt did for me by flying me to England and Germany. Now, though, I realize how much my aunt really tried not to make the remainder of the trip focused around the crash. That would have been understandable, as the news coverage was pervasive, and there was still the air of disbelief. However, she focused on comforting us and on making my trip special, enjoying the remaining time we had together (and believe me, there were a lot more hugs afterward, too). I was most thankful that my aunt, my godmother, whom I love so dearly, was not on that flight and that we would have more adventures together (and I wish for more to come— Sweden, maybe?)

ORDINARY EVERYDAY ADVENTURES

While some experiences are notable, sometimes it's the more subtle ones that leave a lasting impression. The everyday activities can seem like an adventure, especially to a kid. Each summer day was a day of possibility. Days filled with climbing trees, reading books for the summer reading program, lemonade stands, and pick-up games: "Red Rover, Red Rover, Send Robbie right over," if we had enough players. Other times, it was Ghost in the Graveyard. Once it got dark enough for the lightning bugs to start twinkling, we began chasing them. And yes, when we were thirsty, we drank right from the green garden hose (and got in trouble for often forgetting to turn it off!). "Did you turn the hose off?"

I look back now nostalgically at how we would spend our time, and I appreciate the freedom and how safe we felt just hanging outside with other kids, with no tablets, cell phones, or social media. Instead, we had a group of neighborhood kids, and together, we climbed the dirt to play King of the Hill. The older, stronger ones lobbed rotten apples down upon the rest of us or tried to bean us with one as we hid amongst the apple tree branches. They shared my fear of kicking the ball too hard and it ending up in Mr. Terry's yard. He had no patience for us and would quickly come out and shout if we overstretched. I was convinced his wife, with her wily gray hair and scowl, was definitely a witch, and we avoided the couple at all costs.

We'd arrange kickball or baseball games on the fly in the empty lot we called "the field." We rode our bikes down the hill to the IGA and would head back to the bakery to ask for a free cookie. Then we'd ride over to Bound to Stay Bound, the book bindery, on the weekends when the parking lot was empty and hit tennis balls against the wall. I can't imagine how many of our tennis balls were on the roof of that place.

Near the end of grade school, my friends and I would wear our coolest clothes to the roller rink. My favorite was a navy t-shirt that said *Another One Bites the Dust* in white letters underneath my red satin jacket that I wanted so badly that I saved chores and babysitting money to pay for 1/2 of it. We'd have our parents drop us off at the Eight Wheeler roller rink, meeting up with other school friends and then skating around to see who else was there. We'd watch with envy those who were asked by a boy to skate the Moonlight with the Disco ball, even more envious of those girls who could skate backward with a partner and make it look so good. I can picture the rink, how we'd go around and stop suddenly at an opening in the wall to hop out and catch up on gossip. I recall the smell of the fried food in the snack bar and the disinfectant from the rental skates, and it all brings back such nostalgia for simpler times, of happy memories, with giggling friends, trying to look and act older, like a teenager.

And there were times of much-needed solitude. Before I realized I was an introvert and needed some alone time to recharge... I remember lying in the grass on windy days, watching the clouds race by, watching for recognizable shapes, climbing a tree and observing the world below, or taking a book up with me and losing all track of time with whatever series I was into that day. The lazy days of summer made for beautiful childhood memories.

I remember the times we were invited along with family friends who owned a boat. How fun it was to go out on the lake and watch everyone take turns water skiing or tubing. You could feel the variances in the water on your legs as you went through a warm patch or a frigid patch of water, sometimes being tickled by a little tangle of seaweed. Then, when our turn was over, we climbed back in the boat, dripping wet and cold, wrapping the towel around us and feeling exhilarated by the ride. Standing and drying off, we tried to keep our balance as the next person went out, and the boat sped up again. Noticing the mesmerizing arc of the water spray behind the boat and the waves created that rhythmically rocked it while my brother was on the lookout for Jaws lurking below the surface.

These everyday adventures were such a memorable part of my childhood, something to look forward to, and also comforting rituals in that I mostly knew what to expect. I look back on these experiences and am grateful for the ease and the sense of belonging and for the friends who created these memories with me.

"Life is either a daring adventure or nothing."
—Helen Keller[20]

NEW YEAR'S ADVENTURE

When the decade changed from the 1980s to the 1990s, I was in the Soviet Union—with the college basketball team—and my 70-year-old grandmother. We spent New

---

[20] Keller, Helen. *The Open Door*. Doubleday, 1957.

Year's Eve in a hotel in Moscow, under the close super-vision of our tour guides, eating unfamiliar foods and drinking more vodka than college kids should be drink-ing. It was part of a foreign trip that my dad, as the col-lege men's head basketball coach, organized once every four years so that any basketball player would be able to experience a foreign country during their college years.

Many of his players were first-generation college students; many grew up in small farming communities, and this was an invitation to see the world anew beyond the basketball court.

Dad started arranging these trips in the late 1970s, and they included some scrimmages and meals with lo-cal teams. It gave the players on both sides of the court a chance to get to know each other and learn how the games were played abroad, across language barriers and nationality, but ultimately illuminating how similar the players were. The itineraries he chose also sprinkled in some standard guided tours, sneakily ensuring some cul-tural exposure while satisfying Dad's own love of history.

The trip I was lucky enough to join was a combina-tion of France/Belgium/(then) USSR visiting the cities of Paris, France, Antwerp, Bruges, and Moscow. Before agreeing that I could go, my dad also invited my grand-mother on the trip so we could room together, and I'd have a "chaperone" for when Dad was busy with the team. At the time, I wasn't exactly thrilled that I was not going to be able to roam freely and do my own thing. But in looking back, how many kids can say they've been to places such as these with their grandmother?

She was such a good sport, keeping up with us running all over the place on cobblestone streets with her little sensible shoes and polyester pull-on pants. She was always agreeable and up for whatever the group wanted to do and where they wanted to go. I am so thankful to have had that experience with her—we reminisced and talked about our adventures on that trip a lot over the years.

There are many things I remember from that trip, starting from saving for the trip itself. Dad had arranged a shoot-a-thon, where all the players would spend an afternoon shooting 1,000 free throws and got sponsors per basket to help defray the costs. Since I was going, I asked if I could do the shoot-a-thon, too. I was never much of a basketball player, but I managed 382 free throws (some were granny shots when my arms got tired). In the end, I was still a little short on money; my grandmother helped pitch in.

We started our trip in Belgium, and I remember bonding with one of the players who I had been in an art history class with, thinking we'd never use what we were learning, much less remember it. And suddenly, there were columns everywhere—"Look—Ionic, Doric, Corinthian!" and for the remainder of the trip, we'd shout out the type of column any time we spotted one, racing to see who could name it first. Our humorous tour guide showed us around the town center, describing the history of the statue with a man with his arm cut off on the fountain, and took us through Peter Paul Rubens' house. I was surprised by how attentive the players were, especially after grumbling that they had to see "historical stuff." A win for Dad!

While we were not of drinking age in the US, we were in Europe, so the chaperones had their work cut out for them—many a blonde beer was consumed in Belgium. And the medieval city of Bruges was like something out of a fairy tale. We have a couple of good photos of the group on a stone bridge, and when I look at them, it brings me back to that wonderful city.

In Paris, we saw the National Armory and Napoleon's crypt and climbed up to see the view from the top of the Eiffel Tower at night. But my biggest memory was going on a pilgrimage to find Jim Morrison's grave in Pere Lachaise Cemetery. I was determined to go on an afternoon off by myself, but a couple of other players found out where I was going and wanted to go too. As soon as we got into the cemetery, we realized what a hilly, windy, and complete maze it was. It was so old, not laid out in any logical fashion, and not marked. We got in there, and (this was before you could find it on the Internet) some of the guys realized it was going to be a hunt and wanted to leave. I stated confidently that I would find it within an hour, and I just followed my instincts, and off I went. I am proud to say I was able to find it within 30 minutes. The disbelief that we found it and the solemnity of being where he was buried was an overwhelming feeling. We took photos of the gravestone (the statue head had been stolen by then) and of the offerings other fans had left: lighters, cigarettes, letters, coins. As we passed the lighter from the grave around and each had a smoke, we paid homage together. On the way back to the hotel, one of the guys tried jumping the turnstile in the Metro to avoid paying the fee and wiped out. The hilarity that ensued snapped us out of our solemn reverie and back to the antics of being a group of teenagers exploring Paris. What a memory.

We did not know what changes were on the horizon, the upcoming dissolution of the USSR, and that we were there at the end of an era. The few experiences that stick out in my mind were seeing Red Square and all of the children in their fur coats, fur hats, and boots scurrying along atop inches of ice while we struggled to find our footing. Everything was organized and arranged for us; we were not allowed to stray from the group, and our tour guides instilled a sense of panic in us, knowing how closely they (and we) were being watched and monitored.

I took Russian during my freshman year of college (hard language) and have been fascinated by the Soviet Union since seeing the movie White Knights with Baryshnikov. And the one thing I wanted to get while we were there was a CCCP (USSR) red flag. We had been told by our travel agent before we left that people would recognize us as Americans and come up and ask "to trade." Usually, they would trade our gum or chocolate for their collector pins, and we were told to bring these over specifically for trading if we had room in our suitcase. They would ask to buy dollars; they would ask for Levis, for watches, and big-ticket items. And cigarettes were a hot commodity—that could get you something much better...like a flag.

We had been there for a couple of days, and I had yet to get my flag, but one night, as we left the Moscow Circus, I was approached by a man a little older than me asking to trade. I said I only wanted a flag. He asked, "What do you have?" A carton of cigarettes and a lighter later, I had my flag, which I proudly displayed on my dorm room wall for the rest of college and a few years beyond.

What I remember most about the people was the pink cheeks, the curiosity and trepidation, an undertone of being watched, a veil of fear, and a continual awareness of surroundings. I saw this among the staff that were in the hotel during our evening celebration on New Year's Eve. We had a party that had been arranged for us with specific allowed guests that included our guides. It was in a hotel meeting room where they had set up a banquet table and a dance floor with a DJ. I remember how intently the tour guides watched as the food was presented, and with each course that was served, they announced what it was. Many of the things went untouched—caviar, borscht (which I actually loved), and other foods were left on the table. I'm sure the team would have preferred a hamburger or pizza, although they had become quite accustomed to ordering a Fanta since Coke was not available.

After the players left the table and were dancing and challenging each other to shots, I noticed that one of our guides, Masha, was surreptitiously wrapping up some of the untouched rolls in a napkin. I mimicked what she was doing and offered her a couple more under the table that I had wrapped. She looked over her shoulder before taking them, and then she explained to me that the food we were given in this show of extravagance was more than her family would eat or even have access to in a month. She told me how she would never be able to own a car and how they had to wait their turn in line on specific days for bread and cheese. I had read about communism, but reading it in a history book is not the same. The realization that people, ones that I now knew by name and face, had lived in communism sunk in. It reminded me of George Orwell's *Animal Farm* and how some animals were more important than others as they drove around in their cars and how they bossed and bullied and instilled fear. She quickly, almost apologetically, assured me how lucky she was because she spoke English and had a good job as a tour guide. I felt sorrow for her and her family and their circumstances, and I felt an overwhelming sense of shame at the good fortune we all took for granted. It was the first time I remember feeling like an Ugly American.

When we left Moscow and said goodbye, Masha presented me with a children's book so that I could practice my Russian. It belonged to one of her kids. I was so appreciative, humbled, and touched by this gesture of kindness from this woman from the other side of the world who had so little but would share with me. Years later, quite recently, I found a small box in my grandmother's things, and in that box were all of the pins she traded for and collected during that trip, ones that I did not remember her having, ones that she must have treasured to have held onto them for the rest of her life.

From time to time, I will hear from someone who went on one of those trips and how meaningful it was to them, one of their best life memories. One of the players' families reached out to my dad after their son died to let him know how important that trip was to their son and how they were so happy he was able to have that experience. I am grateful for my dad and for what he was able to give those players, more than lessons on the court and in the classroom, but those about the wide, wonderful world. We know so little of it being just in our own corner of it, but we are so similar, all humans—playing, eating, discovering about each other.

⁓

REFLECT AND CONNECT

It's your turn to think about some of the adventures you've had over your life so far:

- What was your biggest adventure, and who was part of it?
- Is there an adventure you had that took you by surprise, had an impact, or turned out differently than you thought it might?

- What trips did you take as a child, and who went on them with you?
- Can you share appreciation for someone who sent you on or took you on those adventures?
- What adventure did someone plan for you (or did you plan for someone)?
- What are some of your everyday adventures you remember from childhood, and who was alongside you?
- Are there adventures you had that you now have a different understanding of or perspective of as an adult?
- Ask your kids what adventures they remember from their childhood and what they remember from them (specifically sights, smells, feelings, tastes)

See if you can find some photos and share them and what you remember from those times with your fellow adventurers. Ask if they have some photos you haven't seen that they can share with you. And please, remember to digitize them.

—— CHAPTER 9 ——

GRATEFUL FOR HUMOR

"A day without laughter is a day wasted."
—Grigori Alexandrov[21]

S ometimes things happen and, in the moment, our immediate reaction is embarrassment. It's only in retrospect that we can look back and see the humor.

BEST INTENTIONS

Honest mistakes can result in lots of laughs and stories retold. And many a laugh has resulted from mistaken lyrics. I remember someone in junior high getting into an argument that the Donna Summer song "Love is in Control" lyric was "I cut my finger on the trailer," instead of "I've got my finger on the trigger." While we couldn't google the lyrics back then, you went by ear unless you had an album or cassette that happened to include the lyrics in the jacket. It's such a common occurrence that now when you do google it, you'll find memes and even glassware with some of the gems. "These ants are my

---

[21] Grigori Alexandrov Says Day Without Laughter Is Day Wasted." USSR, Aug. 1956, pp. 22-23.

friends; they're blowing in the wind" is a Bob Dylan gem I discovered when I looked up mistaken song lyrics myself. And while it's great to laugh at these lyrics and wonder how someone could get it so wrong, it's a different situation when it's you who have gotten it wrong.

My elementary school was a new concept in the 1970s when it was built—instead of classrooms, we had an open floor plan, and each classroom was in an unenclosed area separated by moveable dividers and bookshelves that were taller than us but not taller than the teachers. If you stood on a chair or when you grew and moved into the intermediate pod and stood on tiptoes, you could see into the next class. A huge tile floor was centrally located between all of the classrooms that had a big board used as a chalkboard or movie screen and this served as the gathering place for all of the classes in that pod. The anticipation grew when we were called to gather there.

One year, around Christmas time, they had us come to the tile floor for an assembly, and we saw the piano and Mrs. Peebles, the music teacher, standing there next to it, her tiny frame with huge hair and an even bigger smile. We were always excited to see Mrs. Peebles because it meant a special presentation of some kind—a sing-along or musical performance. That was a time of life when we could not wait to sing out songs loudly and proudly; there was no self-consciousness about being out of key; it was a matter of trying to be the loudest you could be. Sometimes, during these gatherings, another music teacher who played the dulcimer and jaw harp would entertain us with "I Wish I Was a Mole in the Ground" or some other similar folk song. This particular day was definitely a holiday-themed get-together that the teachers arranged for us, the rowdy kids, getting more excitable with each passing day, one day closer to Christmas (and Santa!)

As we gathered and began singing some favorites al-together, with Mrs. Peebles leading in her toe-tapping, arm-swaying way, we sang "Must Be Santa," led by a couple of overly eager volunteers; the Christmas mood was spreading. I was excited for Christmas and to be here singing instead of doing classwork. This soon changed for me when they asked me to come to the front. As a shy kid, this was not something that excited me like it did the other kids whose hands had shot up to be called on to lead. When I got there, Mrs. Peebles asked me to start the group off by singing "Joy to the World." "And sing loudly so we can hear you in the back."

I took a deep breath and belted out, as loud as I could, "Jeremiah was a bullfrog, was a good friend of mine! Nev-er understood a single word he said, but I helped him drink his wine!" The piano abruptly stopped, and there was silence. The kids on the tile looked at me in complete confusion. The teacher accompanying me on the piano started giggling, and some of the other teachers who were standing in a group at the back joined in. I didn't understand what was so funny. I had heard that Three Dog Night song so many times at home and knew I had sung it correctly. I was waiting for others to join in and surprised when no one else did. After what seemed an eternity, my cheeks growing pinker and hotter by the second, one of the teachers piped up, "No, Jennifer, not that 'Joy to the World,' the Christmas song."

I had to admit, there in front of everyone on the tile floor, that I didn't know that song, and I shamefully made my way back to my spot on the floor, stepping around those seated and feeling completely humiliated. I don't remember much beyond that moment other than wondering why my parents had not taught me the right one—the one everyone else knew. I told my mom about it when I got home from school, and guess what? She laughed about it too.

In that moment, the laughter was at my expense, and I didn't see the humor, but now I appreciate how comical it was. I guess that says a lot about the music we listened to...more Three Dog Night (and Eagles and Jim Croce) and less of the traditional Christmas carols, which we all ended up learning anyway, so I'm thankful to my parents for the music they chose to play in our home and grateful for giggles I've gotten when I have shared that story.

LAUGHS FROM CHILDHOOD

What we remember about our childhood friends from our young years is usually in a hazy cloud and, through the lens of developing minds, hard to recollect with certainty and more impressions. What I recall most about my best friends from when I was little is that it seemed whenever I made a good friend, they moved away. I do have some distinct memories about a few of the times we had together before they moved. I wish I had kept in better touch with them, and I wonder where they ended up and what they are doing now. What I remember is how free it felt to play, to act, to laugh without fear of being embarrassed or worrying about fitting in or saying something wrong. It was a time of doing, being, feeling, exploring, adventuring, and absorbing. We just wanted to hang out and invent worlds of make-believe. I certainly feel grateful for the fun and imagination they brought to my life when I was so young.

One of these early friendships was with a girl, Julie, who lived down the street. Because she lived at #7 and we lived at #19, she was about five houses down on the same side of the street. It meant I could go down and play there without having to be accompanied by an adult or babysitter. Julie sounded funny to me—she and her family had moved to my town from Texas and had what I later learned was a strong Southern accent. They had funny speech patterns and said funny words I had never heard of, like "commode." I loved listening to her family talk and her younger brother whine and tattle on her in that Southern twang.

Julie didn't live there long; they moved away probably before I was in 4th grade, but I still remember how hard we laughed together. Not only about funny Southern words but pretty much everything. We were always busy creating something. I remember our library we set up in her house. We carted all the books from their upstairs to the basement to reside on our library shelves through multiple trips up and down the stairs. We became hysterical when her mother demanded to know, "Where did all my books go?" We laughed together at cartoons. She introduced me to that I hadn't seen before, like Bugs Bunny and Roadrunner with Wile E. Coyote. We laughed when we bested the older boys from across the street one snowy day. It was the first snow day I remember having, and we spent our day off building a snow igloo. It was an impressive structure because our igloo protected us from the neighbor boys when they started pelting snowballs at us. We were able to outsmart them with our pile of premade snowballs and we laughed, and laughed when we threw them out of the "window" we'd molded. After they had used their few up, they gave up and ran off. We were victorious!

Julie's house was the first house I had a sleepover in. I was so entertained by her family, listening to them and watching what they liked to do, that I did not have the chance to get homesick. I remember watching *Hee Haw* in the basement with her, sharing a LazyBoy chair together we had slid close to the TV so we wouldn't miss anything, so close that I was sure we were going to hurt our eyes, with her family watching on the couch behind us. I was always a little bit intimidated when they watched with us. They were very strict parents, and I remember her bedtime was earlier than mine. When we got up into her tall and frilly canopy bed, we giggled for hours and had to be reminded more than once that it was past our bedtime.

What I remember most about my first sleepover is the Rice Krispie incident the next morning. We were having breakfast, and she said something that made me laugh as usual. Except this time, my mouth was full, and I tried keeping my mouth closed. The result was Rice Krispies shooting out my nose, which then made me sneeze... and then even more shot out. I was so embarrassed and thought her dad was going to raise his voice (he was a towering presence of Southern-ness). I grabbed a napkin and started hurriedly cleaning up the mess as best I could in the silence, and then he burst out laughing, which made her brother Douglas laugh, followed by Julie, and then her mom and I joined in.

Sitting around that table laughing with adults was the first time I remember seeing an adult as a person with a sense of humor and not as a parent or authority figure. Giggling together softened the wall between adult and child and made me feel connected. Looking back, I appreciate that realization. It was surprising and offered a new viewpoint. I'm thankful that an early friendship was so sweet, so unencumbered, and memorable, even now. I wish we would have kept in touch better.

We were pen pals for a little while, but we were young and couldn't write much in letters. From what I can recall, Julie was not into the letter writing as much as I was. The mailbox would be empty for days, whereas when I received a letter, I would write back immediately. I found it exciting to use my Ziggy or Joan Walsh Anglund stationery. Our letter writing soon fizzled, and we lost touch. My mom didn't keep in touch with her mom either, so I don't know where Julie ended up, but I'm glad for these early experiences of a friendship, where what I remember most is laughing our heads off. I hope wherever she is, she hasn't lost that Southern twang, big sparkly smile, sense of fun, or her imagination.

~

"A good laugh overcomes more difficulties and dissipates more dark clouds than any other one thing."
—Laura Ingalls Wilder[22]

SURPRISING LAUGHS

The time I spent with my second Brazilian family was over the summer holidays, which is December–February there, instead of what we are used to in the Northern Hemisphere. Part of the time that I lived with them was spent at their summer home in the Aldeia Beach area. I have fleeting memories of what the house looked like. There was a pool and a sauna. My Brazilian father showed me how to pull eucalyptus leaves and add them to the hot coals and then pour water over them. The resulting steam would be infused with the eucalyptus, and oh, how refreshing it was to breathe that in. I remember the doors being open and feeling a part of my surroundings, amongst the trees and green, as if the house and the surroundings were one. The area we were in was a bit secluded, like a jungle, woodsy, with great paths to

---

[22] https://www.pbs.org/wnet/americanmasters/10-of-laura-ingalls-wilders-most-inspiring-quotes/16174/#:~:text=%E2%80%9CThe%20real%20things%20haven't,courage%20when%20things%20go%20wrong.%E2%80%9D

explore. One path through the trees led to a massive expanse of black rocks with a view of never-ending ocean waves where sea and sky met. I remember that it was a peaceful place where I would often venture and just sit in wonder, marveling at the view and the difference between the views of home and the views this magical place offered as if it were a dream.

My middle sister in my second family, Fernanda, was the one I became the closest to. She was easy to talk to, funny, sweet, kind, and caring, and I felt she was interested in me as a person, not an American novelty, but truly as a sister. She felt that way to me too (and still does). She was helpful in making sure I was continuing to learn, as at this point, I had been in Brazil for about four months and I could understand much more than when I arrived. I was able to carry on a childish conversation but was still learning new words and customs every day.

One afternoon, she and I went for a walk, exploring, maybe getting some exercise, or getting away from the other sisters. Four girls in one household is a lot. We were walking on the path in the woods, just chatting away when we started to hear some strange sounds: rustling, a low moaning, bellowing sound, almost what I imagined to be prehistoric. We continued walking, but the sounds became more frequent, and we started to get scared, imagining what kind of monsters were lurking in the woods. We made our way from the woodsy path to the dirt road in hopes we were averting the "monsters." Once we were on the road, there was a sense of relief until suddenly Fernanda screamed, "VACA!" and bolted off, running faster than I had ever seen her move. I was stuck to the spot there on that dirt road, wondering what had just happened. I tried to remember what vaca meant, "Vaca, vaca, vaca—hmmmm"? And then it hit me, "Oh—cow!" And then I heard that bellowing sound again, booming behind me, and I turned and saw not one monster but a whole herd of angry horned cattle storming down the road toward me, kicking up dust as they raced in a pack.

The fear and adrenaline kicked in, and I started running as fast as my legs would go, not worried about catching my breath or a stitch in my side but running for my life from this group of vaca. I was pretty far behind Fernanda at this point; she had a head start, and I didn't know where we could go to escape them. I just kept running, hearing the snorts and gallops behind me. The road turned, and as I followed it, I could see a little shack up where Fernanda was headed. I kept going, arms pumping, legs racing, afraid to look over my shoulder to see how close they were gaining on me, visions of looming cattle behind me. I saw Fernanda go into the hut, and she and a man stuck their heads out and screamed at me, Vai! (Go!) As I came up on the hut, the man stuck his arm out. I grabbed his hand, and he yanked me to safety as the herd stormed by. We stood in that hut and watched as the cattle continued on, racing to who knows where. Maybe they thought they were racing to their freedom?

We stood there as they stampeded by, catching our breaths. Then we both burst out laughing, a combination of disbelief and relief. I felt indebted to this man who saved me and fear about ever stepping outside of the hut again. The man helped us make sense of it—apparently, the cattle belonged to a nearby farmer, and they had broken down the fence and escaped. The man radioed and somehow got word to our parents, and our father came to pick us up; two girls completely exhausted, covered in sweat and dust, and still bewildered by the experience. I was so thankful to see him, and it was such reassurance that he came in the car, as I was hesitant to leave the safety of the hut.

We came home and shared the story with our sisters and our mother, which resulted in more surprise and laughs, and requests to retell it, and it was a great story to share at school when the summer break ended. We still laugh about it today and believe me; I will never forget the Portuguese word for cow.

~

"There is nothing in the world so irresistibly contagious as laughter and good humor."
–Charles Dickens[23]

CONTAGIOUS LAUGHTER

My mother and my aunt have this strange sense of humor where they laugh at human catastrophes. And by catastrophe, I mean any time someone falls, stumbles, or knocks something over like a store display. As the person who stumbled is mortified, my mom is just overcome by

---

[23] Dickens, Charles. *A Christmas Carol*. Chapman & Hall, 1843.

fits of giggles. This was often embarrassing for me as a kid. I felt very self-conscious when she'd laugh because we know it's not nice to laugh at someone else's clumsiness.

Once, I was with my mom at the shopping plaza in town on an especially windy day. As we were going into Kline's department store, a man's toupee blew off, and he was chasing it as it blew and rolled across the parking lot. It took a moment to realize what I was seeing. The man was in hot pursuit of what looked like a furry animal. He seemed to be trying to chase it without calling too much attention to himself or the toupee. My mother started laughing loudly, cackling, and I know he heard her laughing by the glare he shot our way.

When my mom and aunt visited me in Brazil, the glass doors were so clean that my aunt accidentally walked right into the glass door at full speed. She hit so hard that she fell backward, a large bump later erupting on her forehead. I ran to see what the noise was and found my mother not helping her sister up but instead on the ground in a fit of laughter at my aunt's expense. Thankfully, my aunt was not too offended since she is not only familiar with but shares that sense of humor. Unfortunately, this laughter is also somewhat contagious, and once it starts, it is hard for either of them to control and impossible for those around them not to join in.

I don't remember my grandmother having this sense of humor, and it's not a trait that I have. My daughter recently relayed that she was on a weekend retreat and couldn't hold back her laughter when someone slipped down the stairs. Perhaps it's genetic and skips a generation.

Whatever form laughter takes, be it silly or contagious or reliving tales, it's a great stress relief. Humor bonds us through shared laughter and the endorphins flooding our systems. I look back, and I'm grateful for the early experiences, and when I think of these memories, I smile.

~

REFLECT AND CONNECT

In thinking back to childhood laughter...

- When did you make an honest mistake, and who was there to laugh alongside you? (Or let you know about it and laughed at you?)
- When did someone make you laugh to the point of tears (or maybe even peeing your pants)?
- What was a time when you couldn't realize the humor in the moment, but looking back, you find it funny?
- How has the humor shared between you and someone else changed your relationship or perspective?
- When has someone sharing humor with you provided much-needed solace or broken the tension?
- Whose laugh is so contagious for you that when they start laughing, you do too?

Reach out and share these humorous remembrances, and find out if they thought it was as funny as you did— or even more so.

CHAPTER 10

GRATEFUL FOR BELIEF & POSSIBILITY

*"If you have just one person believe in you, you'll
always find your way." —Sarah Dessen*[24]

W hen we are young, we feel like we can do anything; our superheroes are real. This tends to
diminish as we age, as we encounter doses of
reality and responsibilities which can feel like enormous
boulders are in our way or the fear of failure prevents
us from moving forward. Sometimes, we need reminders
that our dreams are possible. The feeling of possibility
can fuel us and initiate momentum to lead us forward
in new directions. Sometimes, these feelings resurface
in adulthood through a mentor, who can help us see the
road ahead, reminding us of our strengths and guiding us
in formulating a plan. And while, as adults, we recognize
and label our mentors, it's easy to forget that moments
of guidance happened in our childhood, too. People that
served in these roles weren't necessarily called a mentor or teacher, but it was through the examples of those

---

[24] Dessen, Sarah. *Someone Like You.* Viking, 1998, p. 180.

around us who maybe, even unknowingly, gave us this gift—a sense of possibility.

~

NEIGHBORLY EXAMPLE

I have wanted to write a book for as long as I can remember. I wrote in journals and crafted my own little books. Diaries were often a gift I received for Christmas presents, the ones with the little locks, so worried I'd lose the keys and I'd have to leave it unlocked, and someone would get access to my "secrets." I had a variety over the years: a Holly Hobbie one, a Garfield one, a Miss Piggy one was a particular favorite, and it had different colored pages inside. I loved writing and filling them up with thoughts, crushes, what I'd gotten up to that day, and little stories. Like many of my friends, I devoured *Encyclopedia Brown*, *Little House on the Prairie*, and Judy Blume books by authors who seemed so elusive. If only we were in New York or another big city, we might have had an author visit. We could not simply google a favorite author like we can today and find their website. We couldn't instantly see photos of them, learn about their favorite things, connect with them on social media, discover what they were working on next, or feel like we knew them. Our heroes then were completely inaccessible, and we had to rely on them appearing in a spotlighted article in our Weekly Readers or seeing them on a news segment or maybe a topic of study at our weekly library program.

Growing up, though, we had a neighbor family with four kids who were all older than me but willing to engage with a (probably bothersome) neighbor girl. There was the cool oldest sister who could drive, wore shiny lip gloss, and sometimes babysat. Then there was the creative sister who was in dance and theater and often allowed me to join in her make-believe adventures—imagining we were ruling royalty over some faraway land. The older brother was an athletic, stand-up-to-anyone, natural leader. He intimidated me, but I loved being included in any neighborhood fun he planned and would join in even if I knew I shouldn't (like one activity that involved ants, a magnifying glass, and sunlight that resulted in a popping sound!) The youngest son was closest in age to me, and he was quiet but fierce on the soccer field. I was always glad when he was on my team. The mom taught aerobics and was artistic and was often available if I ever needed anything, especially after school before my mom got home. I felt comfortable to go knock on the door and ask if I needed something or a ride somewhere; she was always welcoming.

My first impression of the father was that he was quiet and not as much of a presence as the mom or the kids, but in the background. I later learned that he had an important job—he was the superintendent of schools. And while this felt like a novelty to have the boss of all of the principals and all of the teachers as a neighbor, the thing that was the most influential to me was what he did in his time away from the school district. He was an author, and his book, *Clyde Monster*, was a tale about a little monster child afraid of humans hiding under his bed. I remember reading the book and thinking how funny it was that monsters might be afraid of us! I loved looking at the pictures and their dream-like quality, and it was easy to identify with Clyde. But even more surprising to me than enjoying the book was the feeling of awe that this person I knew was a real writer! That he, my neighbor, created this story that I held in my hands. We got to actually hear about it, the story, and about being an author when he came to our school to read it during an assembly. I felt so proud to know him, and writing suddenly felt attainable.

Later, he wrote another book, *Tyler Toad and The Thunder*, which also dealt with childhood fears. *Tyler* was also released as a giant coloring book, with giant pages you had to set out on the floor to color because the book was so big! He later adapted this story into a play that was performed in ours and nearby towns. While I enjoyed these stories as a child, I have an even deeper appreciation for them as an adult, how the approach skillfully validates common fears and how relatable the characters are for kids. Mostly, I look back with a deep appreciation for Dr. Crowe's example. He inspired a sense of possibility that I never perceived when I was younger, but I now realize his example showed that you can choose to define yourself in more than one way—to have a full-time job, the one you are known for, while still being able to pursue a dream and find success at both. A sense that a "normal" neighbor and someone I knew could be an author and playwright modeled for me that it wasn't beyond the realm of the possible. It made me feel like I may be able to do it someday, too. Also, it reinforced that authors are regular people, even people who live across the street. Thank you, Dr. Crowe, and also to Mrs. Crowe, who always answered the door when the girl across the street needed something, be that a cup of sugar when I was baking cookies or a stamp for a letter to one of my many pen pals, you were a comfort and a true sense of what a neighbor is all about.

~

CHANGING TIMES

Can someone you have never met infuse you with a sense of possibility? I assert they can, and the actress Marlo Thomas did for me.

Going to grade school in the 70s, it was common for moms to stay at home—most of my friends' mothers did. But we were beginning to sense a shift as the decade progressed and more mothers entered the workforce. Looking back, I realize how much something Marlo Thomas created and shared with children across the country influenced not only me but probably many kids during that era. She made me believe it was possible for me to be anything I wanted to be.

Free to Be You and Me started out as a book and a record of short stories centered around the theme that anyone can achieve and that we are not limited by gender stereotypes. Famous stars of the time joined her in recording songs and reading the parts. A TV show soon followed that must have been made into a filmstrip for schools because that is how I came to see it.

Watching *Free to Be You and Me* was a rare treat for us at Eisenhower Elementary, reserved for special occasions, maybe once or twice a year, that everyone looked forward to and begged to watch. Watching a segment or two of *Free to Be You and Me* was either a reward for when we had behaved exceedingly well, or all finished our SRA cards for the month (remember those color-coded reading cards by the Science Research Associates?), or if we had one of our special Discovery Days, it was a favorite activity.

One of the favorite skits was the Babies. Everyone laughed hysterically and loved the baby puppets voiced by Marlo and Mel Brooks as they tried to figure out if they were a girl baby or a boy baby in the hospital nursery. And the act "William Wants a Doll" normalized boys wanting to play with dolls and offered that it might mean that William wasn't a sissy but rather that he wanted to be a good dad someday. Big, strong football player Rosie Grier let us know that it's alright to cry, and Dudley Pippin's experience with the principal revealed that it's ok to show your feelings, to be upset, and to confide in grown-ups and that those grown-ups would listen, believe, and help you.

The segment that I always hoped we got to see was a retelling of the myth of Atalanta, a fast female runner who could not only keep up with the boys but who beat most of them. It gave me an understanding that I was equal and could compete with the boys and that I could speak up for myself and what I wanted. It was ok to run as fast as I could, to try my best and not hold back as I was prone to do, to save someone else the embarrassment of losing.

It was the beginning of the women's lib, and Marlo created something that felt inspiring and approachable for both boys and girls at the time. Not only was the content funny, the songs catchy, and the characters relatable, but the message was so meaningful and full of infinite possibilities. So, thank you to the young Marlo Thomas, who touched so many little girls' lives at such a pivotal time in history. You made girls believe they could do anything, that they didn't have to be pretty young things but could be whatever they wanted, that they didn't have to win the hand of a prince to be happy but could find it in themselves.

UNEXPECTED ENCOURAGEMENT

I was a shy child and would often struggle to initiate conversations with people. Then, in second or third grade, I discovered the popular phenomenon of autograph books. I thought they were the best invention because they gave a reason and an excuse to talk to someone. I had everyone sign my autograph books. I think it got to the point where I bordered on obnoxious about having people sign my book. I know that I asked my dad's basketball players to sign one when they came to our house for the end of the season celebration. I asked neighbor-hood kids, classmates, and even my parent's friends. I still remember what one of them wrote, Mrs. Marchetti, because it was something I was surprised and touched by and looked back on for many years. What she wrote made me feel like maybe there was something special about me...

Chase your dreams, you can do whatever you want in life because you are Jennifer.

Like Jennifer was something magical to be. She didn't know what it meant to me, but I still remember her handwritten message of belief and encouragement on the light blue pages of my Ziggy autograph book.

My dad gave me similar encouragement recent-ly when, out of the blue, he said, "You should write a book—you have a lot to say, and you're a good writer." His expressing belief in me was the catalyst I think I had been waiting for my whole life. It sparked the little fire of courage that needed to surface so I could complete this. Sometimes, just a few words we've received (or given) can give that boost and make an impact. How wondrous that is.

～

CREATIVE ENVIRONMENTS

Another early friendship from elementary school was with Kristen. I loved going over to her house because it was a den of life with lots of colors and plants, and

the whole environment exuded creativity and possibility. Her family was imaginative, intelligent, kind,
fun, loving, welcoming, and very individualistic. They
didn't care what the norm was. During a time of strict
Mr. So-and-So and Mrs. So-and-So, her parents asked
their children's friends to call them by their first names.
Wow—did I feel grown up (although weird) being able to
do that. Sleepovers at their house were a totally different
experience. There usually was no junk food, but healthy,
organic food before it was a "thing" and widely available.
Bedtime was not strictly enforced. We were trusted to
go to bed when we were ready and tired, which was usually around the time when the parents went to bed too.
While their house might not have been the most organized, it certainly was the most fun, with glorious piles of
interesting things, full of art supplies and machine parts
that were exploration for the senses. We often played
outside in the yard or in the back sunroom, where the
windowed walls streamed in sunlight and moonlight.

Her mom was our Girl Scout leader for a while, and
she brought fun to every meeting. She was a calm presence, with kind eyes, a beautiful laugh, and natural. For
some reason there wasn't the normal girl squabbling
when she was around. She just wouldn't give that non-
sense any time. And when she talked to you, she talked
to you like a person, like your ideas mattered and what
you had to say was important, and there was a level of
respect for you as an individual, which was not common
at that time. I felt free when I was there, not having to
worry about how I was presenting myself or what I was

wearing. It was okay if I had spilled ketchup on my shirt at lunch, and you were accepted for exactly who you were.

They had the first home computer I had seen, a TRS-80, as both parents were engineers, and her parents encouraged creative thinking and problem-solving. I remember we had a sleepover there with another friend, so there were three of us, and we were putting on shows while asking her mom to judge the winner. We performed some of our routines, and then the other guest hurt her foot and said we'd have to stop our performance. Her mom would not have it and encouraged her to find a different way to perform.

After thinking for a couple of minutes, she went "on-stage." Instead of dancing on her feet, she created a little stage on a book and danced with her fingers (pretending to be legs). She had a little napkin wrapped around the "legs" for a dress. We loved the performance and were cheering when she won first place. I love how her parents encouraged inventiveness, thinking up new ways to do something. The experience of being there felt like there just felt like a boundless source of ideas that would be praised and encouraged for their possibility.

I still remember the gist of Kristen's senior quote because it was punny and clever, like her and her family. It was something along the lines of "They say the meek will inherit the world; the question is, do I want the whole world?" It makes me smile every time I think about it.

I also want to thank them for later saving and adopting my cat (THE Cleopatrick) when my parents got a dog that did not play nice with Cleo, and I had found out I was allergic to cats. Cleo lived with them for the rest of his days, and they gave him the possibility of a long, full life, full of land to roam and lots of love. Thank you, Kristen, and thank you, Trina and Bob, for providing a haven of creativity, expressiveness, and possibility.

~

INSPIRING ADVISING

College was filled with possibilities, too. When I went in to meet with my college advisor for the first time, I was nervous as a transfer student about how far behind I was and all that I'd need to do to catch up. I was also feeling awkward about the fact that I had known him in a non-advisor context as I grew up running around the campus—soccer games and college functions. I have vague memories of a cabin at the lake with a big tin tub filled with apples bobbing in water and watching him and other grown-ups dunk their heads, of tagging along with my mom shopping for bulk items in the health food store his wife-owned, and of his sons attending that confirmation class with me. But most of all, I was unsure of my future and how to map it out. He was the Journalism advisor. I suppose I expected a detailed class-by-class inventory of how much I'd have to make up. So, I was surprised when his first question was very calm and curious, "So, if you could do anything, what do you want to do with your life?"

But I was even more surprised with his reaction to my response that I wanted to host Entertainment Tonight. He did not react as my parents did, telling me that was an unrealistic thing to hope for. He did not miss a beat—no smirk, no giggle, no roll of the eyes, but rather a suggestion to consider taking a Spanish class if I would be moving to California and some additional classes that would support this dream of mine. He earned my immediate respect and admiration.

Over the next three years, I had him for several classes, and I continually noticed how supportive he was in encouraging his students. There was a magical, understated excitement in the way he engaged with us. He had a phrase he would repeatedly use as a gauge to determine if we were sucking enough marrow out of life—it was "impassioned to the point of anguish," and he urged us to look for moments in literature (and in life) that made us feel that way. Instead of requiring textbooks, his creative writing classes required a student subscription to The New Yorker magazine, and our reading assignments were learning from the masterful authors and sometimes even analyzing Roz Chast cartoons.

As the treasurer of the American Dialect Society, he had a depth of knowledge and love of language that he shared with us. I will never forget having to learn and recite "Cædmon's Hymn" for an assignment, in Olde English nonetheless, which required writing it out phonetically and memorizing and practicing it again and again. Oh, how the classmates bonded over that assignment and the looks we received when spouting out to each other in the dorm or the Campus Center "Nū scylun hergan, hefaenrīcaes Uard" (translation: "Now let us praise Heaven-Kingdom's guardian...") In introducing us to the earliest surviving English poem, he exposed us to history and imparted wonder and appreciation.

His creative writing classes were my favorite college classes. The small handful of students were a tight-knit group who, by following his lead, encouraged and inspired each other. I look back at that time and feel thankful for the experience of being in his classes. He always made me feel like he not only understood my work but was excited by it, and he introduced me to the joy of writing for expression. He was an author many times over, and I have a few of his books, one of which I asked him to autograph, and its place is on the shelf of my most special books.

I found out that he passed away within the last couple of years, and again, another regret that I never reached out to let him know how much I appreciate his influence of my love of the written word. Instead, I will share this with his children and let them know how I will continue to search for and recognize moments where I'm impassioned to the point of anguish in literature and in life. Thank you, Dr. Metcalf.

REFLECT AND CONNECT

Sometimes, what we see in others ignites a spark in us that lets us believe something is possible, and sometimes, someone reflects back to us the possibility they see in us that we do not.

In thinking about the people you have encountered who believed in you or instilled a sense of possibility...

- When did a story someone shared with you resonate and inspire you?
- What did you dream about as a child? Who supported those dreams? How have those dreams changed as you grew up? (Or did they?)
- What were some of the ways you expressed creativity during your childhood?
- Who believed in your dream or introduced you to something that ignited a lifelong interest or passion?
- When did someone you've never met inspire you to believe something was possible?
- When did someone share advice that sparked a new interest?
- When did someone show you a possibility in yourself that you weren't aware of?

"Never underestimate the empowering effect of human connection. All you need is that one person, who understands you completely, believes in you and makes you feel loved for what you are, to enable you—to unfold the miraculous YOU."
—*Drishti Bablani*[25]

---

[25] https://www.goodreads.com/quotes/8540047-never-underestimate-the-empowering-effect-of-human-connection-all-you

—————— CHAPTER 11 ——————

GRATEFUL FOR WISDOM

O ften, the wisdom shared with us as youngsters comes from teachers or first bosses or parents. Because it comes from an authority figure, it's easy for it to go in one ear and out the other. Sometimes, years later, we realize the lessons in what they shared and wonder if maybe we should have listened more closely.

~

"I believe that what we become depends on what our fathers teach us at odd moments, when they aren't trying to teach us. We are formed by little scraps of wisdom." –*Umberto Eco*[26]

LESSONS LEARNED

This realization was true for me with my dad, and the wisdom that he has shared has not been limited to words but seen through his actions. These are some of the words of wisdom and the lessons that I associate with him...

---

[26] Eco, Umberto. *Foucault's Pendulum.* Translated by William Weaver, Harcourt Brace Jovanovich, 1989.

Work hard, play hard. Growing up, Dad juggled school-year teaching and coaching with being a summertime tennis pro; he never took a summer off. Through grading papers, going on overnight team trips, spending long days in the sun running leagues, giving lessons, and stringing rackets in the evenings, I saw dedication, responsibility, and loyalty modeled, both to his family and to his employers and the people he served. But I also saw how he made time for fun—bridge groups with Mom, poker and Risk game nights with friends, tennis matches, and sports, so many sports. It's a balance of work and play, and that balanced quality is one I now delight in seeing in my brothers.

Challenge yourself. Dad was used to teaching Kinesiology and Tests and Measurements, but when the school's curriculum changed and they started teaching a Core series, he was additionally tasked with teaching the Renaissance and Reformation. Even though it was not in his wheelhouse, he immersed himself in Martin Luther, Moliere, Shakespeare, Machiavelli, *Dante's Inferno*, and the like. He was so into the material he was teaching, that once he even asked our server, "Have you read *Tartuffe*?" (which my brothers and I found hilarious.) He made me step outside of my comfort zone by making phone calls to adults to tell them their tennis rackets were restrung and ready for pickup. I hated doing it, initiating conversations with adults (!), but it taught me valuable communication skills at an early age that I'm able to apply every day in my work.

Be disciplined about exercise. Routine is important. As a physical education professor, it makes sense that exercise was a focus, but it's one Dad truly modeled. I think he jogged most every day of my childhood. So many mornings began with me coming into the kitchen, seeing him post-jog, all sweaty, and reading the paper while drinking a huge glass of ice water, waiting to cool off before showering and getting on with his day. Do what you need to do first, and then you have time to enjoy what you want to do. Being so physically active has probably prolonged his life, and it kept him jogging into his 70s. I know I feel better when I'm in a routine and disciplined about exercising first thing in the morning, just like Dad.

Life is made up of peaks and valleys. This is something I heard often: life is a series of peaks and valleys. Sometimes, you're on a peak, and sometimes, you are in a valley and have to climb back up. Sometimes, your opponent is better than you; they were more prepared, or the calls just went their way. As long as you try your best, feel good about your effort. Persevere, continue practicing, and try your hardest. Maybe next time, you will be standing on the peak.

How meaningful words can be. I remember a plaque on his office wall of the Old Irish Blessing. The verse I remember most:

> *May the road rise to meet you,*
> *May the wind be always at your back.*
> *May the sun shine warm upon your face,*
> *The rains fall soft upon your fields.*
> *And until we meet again,*
> *May God hold you in the palm of his hand.*

He loved those words, and the sweetness of them conjures up such a warmth in me. Every time I feel the sun warm upon my face, I think of those words and my dad. I close my eyes, take a deep breath, and soak up the moment and smile. Another quote that makes me think of him is, "The race is not always to the swift, but to those who keep on running." That rings in my ears whenever I feel the urge to quit something.

Thanks, Dad, for sharing these wise words through the years. During difficult times, I find comfort in these words, comfort in the lessons you have shared, and they serve as an anchor for me; sometimes, it's those words that keep me going and bolster me to take the next step.

⌒

"Teaching is the profession that teaches all other professions" –Unknown[27]

IMPORTANCE OF REFLECTING

When I was in graduate school, I took many classes taught by my advisor. As part of her classes, she had a requirement that I found completely aggravating. After every assignment, we had to take a little mini tape recorder and record a reflection about the assignment that we had just completed. We could talk about the things that we found challenging, enlightening, insights we discovered. It was awkward, though, to sit and talk into a tape recorder and know that somebody else was going

---

[27] https://www.teachthought.com/pedagogy/great-best-quotes-about-teaching/

to hear it. Obviously, I complied because it was part of the assignment, but it was an uncomfortable experience for me, and I didn't enjoy it—at the time. But turnabout is fair play, and I respect how she did the same for us by providing responses to our reflections. I enjoyed those responses a lot more.

She returned the assignments with not only our grade but her feedback, and being able to hear it in that way, personal and individualized, was not only helpful, but it lessened any communication errors or misunderstandings. It helped us understand her guidance, what she appreciated about our work, and where we could improve. It was not always just about the content but about our approach to something. Or, she would provide a suggestion: "Hey, you might want to think about this..." It was really impactful. I became more comfortable with this process with each class that I had with her, but I still did not enjoy doing the reflecting and recording those tapes.

After graduating and being out in the working world, I realized how important reflection is in so many aspects of life. Reflection is an important part of not only learning, but feeling and processing and actually part of the whole human experience, any relationship, conversation, or action. Because we need that time to just sit and digest and think through before we can truly reflect back in an honest way and understand the impact. Often if we give ourselves that time to revel in the thinking and processing, additional insights bubble up that lead to new thoughts and ideas. Thoughts and ideas we might not have uncovered had we not taken the time to let it soak in and instead hopped from completing one project right into the next one.

In a workplace, when you finish a project, it's common practice to do a retrospective and identify what went well, what could be improved, and what you might like to do differently next time. But now, when I look back on these required reflections, I realize what she taught wasn't a lesson for class; it was a lesson for life. Reflection applies to any type of growth path or personal challenge, from relationship communication to year-end reviews. Stopping to reflect and think about what went well and what you'd like to improve is a crucial part of learning and evolving.

So, while I didn't appreciate these assignments at the time, I'm so grateful now to her for this lesson. Reflection enhances and allows for a full experience. You can't appreciate something until you reflect on it, just like this.

~

INVENTIVE LESSONS

In fifth grade, I had a teacher, Miss Robinson, who taught lessons in a different way but one that made them stick. One of these I still remember was how she taught us about latitude and longitude. The way she highlighted the difference was when she said latitude, she moved her mouth so it was shaped from side to side, horizontally. She said, "Look, when you say latitude, see how your mouth moves," and she would accompany that with hand gestures. Then she showed us longitude, opened her mouth up and down vertically, and moved her hands the same way. This led to giggles when we practiced and compared our own versions of latitude and longitude mouths with those around us.

But then she surprised us with something else that she called "Miss Robinson lines," which run diagonally. It was kind of a funny thing, but she would always say latitude and do the movement, and then she would do longitude and do the movement with her arms up and down up and down, and then she would throw in Miss Robinson lines, which were diagonal. I actually think she probably put that on a quiz for extra credit: In which direction do Miss Robinson lines run?

But here I am, 50 years later, and I still remember my longitude and latitude, as seen by my mouth and hand movements. Thank you for that, Miss Robinson, for making learning stick and for showing us how interjecting something unexpected, like throwing in a little Miss Robinson line every once in a while, keeps things interesting.

~

"If you could only sense how important you are to the lives of those you meet; how important you can be to the people you may never even dream of. There is something of yourself that you leave at every meeting with another person." —*Fred Rogers*[28]

---

28 *Mister Rogers' Neighborhood.* Produced by Fred Rogers Productions, PBS, 1968-2001.

MISTER ROGERS WISDOM

Mr. Rogers was a fixture of my childhood. I always looked forward to watching his show. I felt like he was talking directly to me, and I felt seen and heard before I knew what that even meant. He taught children everywhere so much, and I was thankful to have his show air every weekday when I was growing up. He reminded us to dream, to imagine; he encouraged us to create worlds of make believe, to learn about others, to be kind and curious. His lessons were thoughtful and slow-paced, not loud and overwhelming, but calm and soothing. One of the things that he taught was to look for "the helpers" in times of trouble or challenge and that you'll always find people helping. And although this has received some backlash in more recent years, as a child, this was an important lesson for me.

As a child, I was prone to daydreaming and would stay behind, lost in thoughts, or would often wander away in stores. I can recall that panic rising when I realized I was lost somewhere, head turning hurriedly from side to side, looking for my mom. I would check a couple aisles over one way and then the other way and know that she had gone ahead while I was lollygagging.

In those times, I'd remember what Mr. Rogers said, and I would look for the helpers, for somebody who had the store vest on or a name tag, and I would go up to them and tell them I was lost. They would usually take me to the customer service desk and announce over the loudspeaker that they had a lost child and for her adult to please come claim her. I was thankful for that advice, and it was acted upon several times. (And still, as an adult, if I'm lost in a city, I look for the helpers in their uniforms in train stations or airports to point the way.)

One other lesser-known example of Mr. Rogers wisdom he modeled when he came to my college to give the commencement address. Mr. Rogers was very diligent about following his routines, and part of his wellness routine was a morning swim. One of the agreements he made with the college prior to his attending commencement was that he could have a private place to swim in the morning so that he could stick to his routine. As the athletic director, my dad was the one to go over and open the swimming pool at 6 a.m. so that he could swim his laps before he started his day and stick around to ensure no one disturbed him (what a cool "job" for my dad!)

The behavior he modeled privately, prioritizing your health and wellness and keeping to your routine, was right in line with the wisdom he shared publicly. And his wise words live on in reruns, movie adaptations, and books. What a legacy!

GENERATIONAL WISDOM

Sometimes wisdom is shared through repeated little sayings, passed down from a grandparent or friend, or something that resonates or rolls off the tongue in a way that makes sense to us. Other times, wisdom is passed down through actions we witness. There are a few sayings and actions shared in my family that come to mind for me...

During challenging times, my mother shares, "My grandfather always said to me, 'Behind every cloud, the sun is shining." This is true. Sometimes, you just need to wait; wait it out for the clouds to dissipate and the sun's warm rays to peek through to brighten your spirit. Wise words carried from one generation to the next (and to the next).

Mom has shared multiple times how surprising, yet touching, her father was on her wedding day. Right before her father was ready to walk her down the aisle, when it was just the two of them, arm in arm, he suddenly got teary and apologized to her. He said that he had spent so much of his life chasing the almighty buck that he lost out on time with his family and in her growing up. A reminder she found meaningful and something to take to heart—life is short, so spend your precious time on those who matter most.

My grandfather may have missed some things, but he shared wisdom through the way he lived. Modeling living a life with gusto, he pursued his passions in his free time—sailing and being part of the Mackinac to Chicago race. He refined his artistic talents through classes at the Art Institute. He got his pilot's license and flew frequently. A continual student of life, he was always learning, experiencing new challenges, pursuing passions. This was wisdom he shared with his family, likely without knowing it.

My grandmother always said, "count your blessings." Usually, this was in response to something I was complaining about. It was usually something someone said or did or did not do. And her response was merely, "Count your blessings." This would frustrate me because I felt like she wasn't listening to me or was minimizing whatever my perceived problem was. In retrospect, I can see that she was reminding me to be grateful for what I did have, changing the focus from the negative to instead shift to something that I'm thankful for. She was wise in her perspective, and anytime I see anything in a shop with "count your blessings" on it, I pause and reframe whatever is going on. I also frequently purchase it—I have to—because it is so Grandma.

My Uncle Dennis was successful both in profession and avocation. A talented artist by nature, he lived life big and had adventures aplenty: snorkeling in the Great Barrier Reef, going to the Rock of Gibraltar, riding camels, and seeing the pyramids of Egypt, deep sea diving in the Red Sea, he traveled everywhere, always yearning for new experiences and always up for a challenge. As much as my father was conservative, his brother Dennis was a risk-taker. He was a successful VP and later executive consultant who would often share his worldliness and wisdom with his eldest niece. Things like "always keep your résumé updated because you never know when a great opportunity is out there; you owe it to yourself to be prepared." "Always look for the next challenge," and "Always ask for more than you want because it doesn't hurt if the answer is no, and sometimes you'll get a maybe or a yes."

We didn't see my great-aunt Mary often, but whenever we were near, she would walk up to us with a big smile, arms outstretched, and proclaim, "Hugs are free!" Words of wisdom with the added benefit of a big ole Aunt Mary hug.

WORKPLACE WISDOM

One of my first jobs was at a life insurance company, and although it was my first job and I wasn't there very long, I still remember wise words from two of the people I worked with there. The first was my boss, who said it was important to always keep one large bill, he suggested $100, tucked away in your wallet. I presumed it was for emergencies, and he said no, that it shouldn't be spent. No matter how tight money got, that $100 bill must stay put because having it and knowing it was there would instill confidence. I don't carry cash often anymore, but for decades, I followed that practice. Even if I'd be down to my last $2, I would not break into that $100, and you know what? It did instill confidence, just to know I had it.

The second set of wise words was from our office manager. She shared advice and modeled behavior for dealing with being a female in a male-dominated office. She may have worked for these men, who strutted their salesmen selves like peacocks around the office, but she would not take anything from those guys. She ran the show and even better to me as an observer; it was evident that they all knew it. If one of them said something to me in a teasing yet derogatory way and I was visibly upset, she followed me into the bathroom (the only place that was private) to have a little talk. During these talks, she urged me to stand my ground, not look down at the floor when they spoke to me. Instead, she cheered me on to hold my head high and give it right back to them. She always looked so put-together, impeccably dressed, with a good, strong red-lipsticked smile that mirrored her interior strength. And through her actions, I saw how to be a capable, confident, and proud woman. I wasn't in that job long before I moved away, and we did not keep in touch. I was surprised and saddened to hear that she was in a serious car accident that left her with permanent injuries that she suffered through for several years before passing away. I regret that I did not have the chance to tell her thank you and share how I appreciated her wisdom, her positive impact, and how I still recall it decades later. When I'm struggling and feeling vulnerable, especially in a male-dominated environment, I like to remember her in those moments, our bathroom chats, and think of her confident and feminine swagger, the one that let everyone know it was she who was in charge. Thank you, Kathy, and I'm comforted by the thought that you shared the same wisdom with your own daughters.

In another early job, I met someone I consider my first mentor, even though that was not her title or defined role. She showed an interest in my professional development and took me under her wing. She encouraged me to come to her when I had a tough situation, and she would talk me through it and role-play. She let me practice with someone safe, guided me outside my comfort zone, and allowed me to make mistakes with her so I was prepared for the real deal. When I came to her with an idea, she taught me to approach proposing it by writing a summary of how it would help and the problems it would solve. She then supported me in proposing it to leadership. Her last piece of advice before I pitched it was to go into that meeting expecting the answer to be yes. I got a yes when I did just that. Thank you, Bette.

~

REFLECT AND CONNECT

In thinking back through lessons you've learned through the words and actions of others:

- What sayings seem to stick with you, or are ones that reflect how you approach life?
- What wise words do you associate with a specific person and always think of them when you hear them?
- Are there wise sayings that were shared that you continue to pass on?
- What are the daily practices you follow because of advice, or behaviors, or traditions someone modeled for you?
- Who believed in you to the extent that they invested in you and shared their wisdom and guidance?

- Was there a time you remembered someone's advice in a troubling situation, and it helped get you out of it?
- When did you last take some time to just reflect (and appreciate)?
- What lesson did a teacher share that you still remember today?

Choose a few from the list that resonate and share your reflections and appreciation for the people whose wisdom had a positive impact on you, or share them with their family or friends. Whose day would not be improved by someone reaching out to tell them how wise they are?

CHAPTER 12

GRATEFUL FOR MOMENTS OF DELIGHT & SURPRISE

M oments of delight enrich our lives in a way that reminds us of the joy we are meant to experience. Sometimes, I am able to recall the awe I felt, how my heart skipped a beat or my lungs a breath, or how I felt in that moment so vividly. These are those magical, serendipitous times we are reminded and amazed by the world and the beautiful things around us. My descriptions here are the best I can remember them, and they are all random remembrances. May you find something that sparks a similar recollection of joy, surprise or delight...

DELIGHTING IN THE MUNDANE

In college, I needed a job, and my parents gave me a deadline. Of course, I let that date almost approach and waited until a little panic and pressure set in. So, the day prior to THE deadline, I opened up the yellow pages and started going down the list. I didn't have to go far before

I found one that I thought might be hiring, a truck stop whose name started with a B, so it appeared near the top of the list. I called to ask if they were hiring, and the person who answered the phone said, "Is this Jennifer?" It turned out to be a friend from high school whom I had lost touch with after graduating and was waitressing there. She said yes, they were looking for a cashier for the 2 to 10 p.m. shift. That sounded perfect to me as it fit in with my class schedule, so I borrowed my dad's car to go fill out an application. When I did, my friend introduced me to the owner's wife (who seemed to be the one you had to impress). Luckily, I was interviewed and hired on the spot. It was a great surprise to see my old friend and catch up, and I looked forward to working when she and I were scheduled for the same shift.

Another person I learned to look forward to seeing scheduled on the same shift was a dishwasher/busboy, Tommy. He was not anyone that I had known, and being from a small town, you know or at least know of quite a few folks. He had a sly grin and was someone who talked back a lot. He was reprimanded frequently by said lady in charge, usually for throwing soapy sponges and horsing around in the back. He would wipe his hands sheepishly on the dirty work apron and apologize, and after she turned around, he'd make a face and then grin at me. He made things a little more interesting at that truck stop. But the best part was at the end of the night. The owners usually sat perched at their table—no one else dared sit there—chain smoking and black coffee guzzling, raising their cup to me to signal they needed a refill, which was one of the cashier's duties, overseeing their empire until well after dinner. When they would finally call it a day and leave, you could feel the energy shift amongst the staff and become much more relaxed, like a collective sigh of relief.

At 10 o'clock, when the shift was over, Tommy would come out from behind the back kitchen counter, untie and remove his apron in dramatic form, and head straight to the jukebox and look at the songs while lighting up a smoke. I don't know why he looked because every night he'd choose the same song, Lou Reed's "Walk on the Wild Side." He'd sway slowly as it started playing, eyes closed, satisfied grin, and then as it picked up, he'd dance with that apron thrown over his shoulder, cigarette hanging out of his mouth. Others would set down the coffee pots and tuck their order tickets in their apron pocket to join in. We'd sometimes try to pretend to do a fancy couple dance, and we'd stumble through, trying to mimic dance moves we'd seen and laugh, and it was just a few minutes of pure joy, this little ritual at the end of the day. He came alive, and the energy was contagious. It didn't matter whether he didn't have a ride home or had been kicked out of his apartment or been told off several times by the truck stop owner's wife. It was all forgotten for those few minutes when the shift was done, and Lou started singing.

I didn't last long at that truck stop, maybe a few months, before finding something a little less, as my mother called it, "seedy." And there are some truly seedy stories I could tell from my short stint there. I don't remember Tommy leaving, he just wasn't there all of sudden, his name not on the schedule. I didn't know his last name or where he went next, and I never saw him again, but I am thankful for his example of finding fun in the mundane and creating an end-of-the-day ritual that let us forget whatever woes of the day and just enjoy the music and moving around, freely, unapologetically clumsily in expansive joy. And I never hear that song without thinking of him.

~

SNEAKY SURPRISE

When I was in second or third grade, all my friends had their ears pierced, and I wanted mine pierced too. Every time I asked my mom, she kept saying I wasn't old enough and that I could get them done when I was ten.

At school, it felt like all the girls were talking about their earring collections and would show off when they had new ones, and it was a conversation I could not be a part of. When I went to friends' houses, I would see their little wire owl earring trees displaying all of their beautiful little studs, birthstones, animals, and flowers, and I was so jealous. But when I repeatedly asked, the answer remained no.

One summer day, after swimming lessons, my mother told me to pack up because we were going home for the day. Usually, I would stay out at the pool after lessons for the rest of the day and come home with Dad, but this day, she insisted I needed to come home. I was not happy, especially because my brothers got to stay out and swim. In the car on the way home, she said she needed to stop by JCPenney's. I was even more aggravated, and then, instead of letting me sit in the car like my pouty little self wanted to do, she said I had to come in with her. I slammed the car door, arms folded across my chest, and stomped behind her into the store. When she opened the glass doors to the vestibule, there was a metal stand-up sign, one that probably was there announcing sales each week that I had never noticed. She told me to look at the sign and tell her what it said. It said "Ear Piercing," and the dates included that day's date!

I looked up at her, and she was smiling a huge smile. I asked if that was for me. She told me it was and to go ahead and get in line. My folded arms quickly dropped to my sides, and her grin was matched by my own as we joined the line. I was excited and couldn't believe I was finally going to get my ears pierced! What I remember most in that moment was feeling astonished that she planned that prank of making me come home so that she could surprise me in an amazing, delightful way.

That hometown JCPenney is still open. I recently went there with my nephew, and I told him and the cashier as we were checking out that I had gotten my ears pierced there so many years ago. Neither were impressed. I smiled, though, as the memories came flooding back of that day and the delightful surprise my mom gave me.

UNEXPECTED BENEFACTOR

On my trip to England to visit my aunt and cousin, I didn't have much spending money. I was a college student and only took with me what I was able to save from babysitting and tutoring. Thankfully, my housing and food were taken care of by my aunt, and I just had to worry about spending money and souvenirs. That went quickly, though, when I found the cousin-approved, non-American looking shoes I just had to have. My GB shoes were black suede lug-soled shoes that I had for many years. I loved them so much I even had them re-soled at least once.

But buying those GB shoes took a huge chunk of my spending money, and I was definitely running low, but I was too embarrassed to say anything to my cousin and aunt about it.

While I was there, my uncle and aunt on my dad's side, Uncle Dennis and Aunt Alma, were visiting England, her homeland, and would be passing through London. Uncle Dennis called my aunt and asked if he could arrange to take me out to dinner while they were visiting. They picked me up at my aunt's flat in Windsor and took me to dinner with a couple who were friends with Aunt Alma. It was my first experience at an Indian restaurant, and it was fancy and fun. I loved how Uncle Denny explained everything I was trying and the ways to dip and enjoy. Aunt Alma and her friends were cracking up, sharing old stories of performing in Spain in their younger years. It was a joyful evening, and I felt very grown up.

Until Uncle Denny brought me back to reality by whispering, "How are you doing for money, Jenn?"

I told him I was okay, and he persisted, wanting to know exactly how much I had left. I thought he wanted me to pay for my dinner and started to worry, so I fessed up and told him how much I had, which was probably 10 or 15 pounds. He told me that he thought that might be the case and passed me a wad of bills under the table, 200 pounds, which was so much money to me and even more than I started out having on my trip. I told him thank you, but that I couldn't accept that, it was too much. He said it was okay. It wasn't from him; it was from Grandma. He said he told Grandma he was going to be seeing me, and she gave him that to give me and that she would be upset if I didn't accept her gift. I reluctantly accepted it, feeling guilty for the relief it offered. I did not have to worry about spending money for the rest of the trip, and I believe I even had some left when I went home. One of the first things I did when I returned was call Grandma to thank her for the money. What do you think she said? She asked, "What money?" I will always remember his kindness; his surreptitious way of getting me to accept it was typical of my Uncle Dennis, generous and full of surprises.

～

"The true delight is in the finding out rather than in the knowing." —Isaac Asimov[29]

---

[29] https://www.blinkist.com/magazine/posts/genius-isaac-asimov-top-quotes

DISCOVERY DAYS

My grade school was ahead of its time with trying new and different ways of collaborative learning. One of the programs the teachers created for us that exemplified this type of learning were special days called Discovery Days. I don't know how often these happened, or if we were told about the first one ahead of time or just arrived at school and were surprised by the changes the teachers had orchestrated. We discovered that the shared spaces (music room, gym, tile areas) had been transformed, each one a rotation we would get a turn experiencing, and each Discovery Day was focused on a theme.

One of the themes was outer space and the music room became the galaxy, the ceiling was now the sky, covered by black paper with stars twinkling, some hanging just out of reach. One room had a huge bubble where we got to sit inside of a gigantic plastic tent that fit the whole class and it was like we were inside of a spaceship. These days were whole sensory experiences, music and sounds, smells from cooking activities wafting through the school, replacing the normal scent of cafeteria food. Another of the themes was prehistoric with huge dinosaur shadows on the wall in the background while a filmstrip played teaching us about prehistoric life, making us feel like we were in a swamp watching the Brontosaurus as they gobbled up plants. The students were so excited to discover what the next activity was and were always on their best behavior so as not to miss one of the rotations on those amazing days of interactive learning.

I was able to see two teachers from my early childhood years recently and was able to talk about and thank them for those Discovery Days. I wanted them to know how important they were to us and how thankful I was to have those experiences and for the effort they and all the teachers put into them. I shared how much we looked forward to them and how delightful and magical they were. My 1st grade teacher looked at me with a smile and said, "They were magical for us, too."

~

HEATHER'S SONG

Talents are often hidden, taking us by surprise when they emerge. In my later grade school years, my parents decided I was old enough for overnight camp. On one of the last nights of camp they were holding a talent show in the dining hall. I loved watching these and had been hearing some of the campers talk about their acts. I had seen them practicing during the week in our free time. Most of the campers were from out of town and I didn't know them before the camp, but there happened to be someone who was from my town and whose father was also a professor at the college with mine. I had known her for a while and did not know her to be any type of performer, so I was not expecting her to take the stage for the talent show. I was amazed by her bravery to walk out there without a group of friends, but by herself. Even more amazing was when she opened her mouth and out came the sweetest voice I had ever heard, with a soulful and angelic a cappella rendition of John Denver's "An-nie's Song."

The room immediately became silent, everyone in the audience mesmerized as she so beautifully captured the feelings of that song. I had never felt an emotional con-nection with that song before but hearing her sing with such feeling, eyes closed and, in a voice that I thought must be what an angel sounds like. It was a beautiful voice that grabbed your soul, one I had no idea she had. I have always had a level of appreciation for her since that moment, remembering the awe and surprise (and goose-bumps) I felt in watching her sing and in looking around at the faces in the audience and seeing a similar reaction. I hope Heather is out there somewhere, still singing, still delighting those who are fortunate enough to hear her.

ARTIST WISHES

In the months leading up to my wedding, a VW commer-cial was out that had a song that I loved. The commercial was one that featured a wedding and even though I was not planning on running away like the bride in the com-mercial, The Graduate-style, I did want this song at my wedding. After some sleuthing that involved calling VW Headquarters, I found the artist's name. But I was not able to find anywhere to buy the CD because it had been a limited run. I found the artist's website—this was in the early 2000s—and wrote a message to the contact ad-dress describing how I went about finding out his name and how I just HAD to have the song at my wedding. Of course, I was not expecting to hear a response.

The next morning, I opened my email to find a message in my inbox, not from his publicist but him, directly. His reply was:

"Then you shall have it. Best wishes, J Ralph"

He had attached the mp3 for me, which I didn't know what to do with (thankfully, my techie colleagues helped me, and we burned it onto a CD for the wedding.) His limited run was re-released in the next couple of years, and I was very quick to buy the CD to support him. What a surprise and a magical moment (and he gained a lifelong fan!)

⁓

"There is no delight in owning anything unshared."
—*Lucius Annaeus Seneca*[30]

REFLECT AND CONNECT

In thinking back on times in your life that you've been the recipient of a surprise or a delightful realization,

- What is a ritual someone shared with you that brought you joy or you felt delighted to be part of?
- Who surprised you by fulfilling a wish you wanted?
- What did they do and in what way was it a surprise? What did that moment mean to you, and how did it change the way you felt about the person?

---

[30] https://www.brainyquote.com/quotes/lucius_annaeus_seneca_133699

- Has anyone shown up at the right time in the right place in support of you?
- What delightful introduction sparked a lifelong interest for you and who introduced you to that?
- What was the best surprise you received?
- Was there a teacher or a class that surprised you?
- What is a hidden talent someone shared, and how did it surprise you?

Share your thoughts and reflections with someone, the people who amazed you, their loved ones or friends. Compare notes, have they done something similar for them too? Is delighting others part of their legacy?

---- CHAPTER 13 ----

GRATEFUL FOR A SENSE OF BELONGING

"The greatness of a community is most accurately measured by the compassionate actions of its members." —*Coretta Scott King*[31]

D
o you remember what you were like as a kid, how you felt you fit in with others? For me, I think the prevailing sense was that I was unseen and not particularly special in any way—very ordinary. Looking back, I think I had a more understated manner to me—once I was told it was like I was a little old lady in a child's body. I remember feeling like I faded into the background, more keen to observe than participate, and that left me feeling unnoticed.

I wonder how often our sense of belonging as a child follows us unwittingly into adulthood. I can recall multiple times when I spent time with someone at a dinner party or girls' night and then later saw them and they had no recollection of me. How embarrassing!

~

[31] https://www.latimes.com/archives/la-xpm-2000-jan-17-mn-54832-story.html

FITTING IN

In grade school, I felt like I was in the nondescript middle of the herd—more of a follower than a leader, not chosen first but usually not chosen last. When recess was organized and not free play, it was stressful to me. That picking teams thing created such anxiety. Two captains were designated, usually the best athletes or loudest students, pointing and choosing until one lonely last kid was left, humiliated at having been the booby prize. In retrospect, it was a kind of cruel way of splitting up into teams, and I hope grade schools no longer do that.

I can picture standing on the blacktop with the empty field of dead grass behind the school that would become a subdivision before I finished junior high. My fourth-grade self was waiting to be chosen for kickball teams, holding my breath. I can see myself jumping up and down with nervous energy and trying to catch the eyes of the team captains, willing them to *please pick me, please pick me.* I was not the fastest, couldn't kick it far enough to make a home run, but generally a pretty safe bet to make it to first or second base; after all, I did play soccer. I remember always wishing to not be one of the last few and sometimes wondering if the captains of the day even knew my name.

I was pretty good when we had four square tournaments. I was (quietly) highly competitive and beat even most of the boys. But when it got to be near the end, and the players who were eliminated and gathered to watch outnumbered those who were left in the game, and it was down to the final group, I became self conscious. I was aware of feeling the eyes on me and I would purposely get out so I could escape being the center of attention. I think my teacher noticed that I would do this—sometimes she'd catch my eye, and I'd look away in shame.

Around this time, there was a boy in my grade who was a little rebellious in that he would talk back to the teacher, and it didn't seem to bother him when he'd get reprimanded for that or being late to class. I remember watching his carefree demeanor and antics with fascination and admired how confident he was. He had broken his leg, and was unable to participate in recess and my teacher suggested that I stay inside and keep him company. He suggested we play this tabletop Carrom set that could be placed on the ground so he could set his leg out straight because the cast was heavy. He taught me how to play and I loved it. Recess flew by. The next day my teacher asked if I could stay in with him again and I jumped at the chance.

It became a daily ritual and one that not only made me more comfortable—I didn't have to worry about trying to find someone to hang out with at recess or the dreaded team selection— but it was fun and something I looked forward to. We kept a running tally of who won in Carrom each day. We had to because we were pretty evenly matched by then. We caught the attention of some others who would have rather stayed in, and when they asked him if they could play, I dreaded the thought of being replaced, but he turned them away. I thought he must have believed I was a worthy opponent, but it also felt like he was sticking up for me. Long after his cast came off, class would be dismissed, and he'd look over and say, "Hey, are you coming?" And he'd hobble over and grab the board to set up. That little ritual in 4th grade gave me an escape for those short times during the day, a sense of having somewhere to go, of being accepted. Thank you, Sheldon.

~

MEMENTO WOES

Mementos can provide a sense of connection to your past and reinforce a sense of belonging. We didn't have smart phones and not many families had camcorders growing up. We didn't get one until the 90s. Instead, we had photos and letters to record the times. I'm particularly sentimental about keepsakes, and I think this is because I've lost them over the years and not just once, but actually on three different occasions. The first was after high school.

I had saved everything when I was growing up and had boxes of it all: swimming ribbons, tennis trophies, certificates for good behavior or most improved student or spelling bee finalist, Brownie and Girl Scout badges, class photos, letters from pen pals, notes passed in class, those cootie catcher fortune-telling things. I had tons of scrapbooks filled with these items. From my year abroad in Brazil alone, I had put together seven scrapbooks of items I'd traipsed home with: photos, drawings, letters, tickets from events I attended. And then I went off to college. At the end of the summer before I left for my freshman year, my mom told me they were thinking of putting the house on the market and asked me to gather up stuff, which was in huge piles on my dresser. I grabbed a big box and slid everything off the top—into the box it went, a glorious mess of papers and knickknacks and all of my collections.

When I came home for Thanksgiving, I went downstairs to my room and asked my mom where my box of stuff was. She asked if I meant the big box with papers on top next to my dresser. When I said yes, the one with all of my scrapbooks and trophies and everything, I saw the horrified look on her face. She broke it to me that in the frenzy to get the house ready to show they thought it was trash and had thrown it away. And it had been weeks ago so there was no use of trying to contact the trash company. It was gone, all gone, in one fell swoop—senior pictures, mix tapes, my coveted autograph books. She was devastated. I was devastated. Newspaper articles with swim team and tennis team match results, all I had collected in my year overseas, relics of the people I had met that I didn't know if I'd ever see again; I no longer had anything tangible from all those years which made it feel like it didn't exist. I felt untethered.

In my remaining college years and in my 20s I became very protective about the stuff I accumulated after losing it all. This time, I had a few boxes, and I made sure I always had them labeled and that I knew exactly where they were stored. At this particular time, that was in the basement in a corner, tucked away nice and safely. One of the treasured possessions in those boxes was a recorded interview with my great-grandmother, my Nana. Born in 1901, Nana was in her 90s by this time, and she was still a little dynamo, vibrant and energetic, as she had walked five miles a day for as long as I had known her, always in loafers and a skirt—I don't ever remember seeing her in pants. She was always very proud of the fact that she had all of her own teeth and would tell you that. Her skin was so soft, and she swore it was due to using Noxzema for decades. She was the matriarch of the family, holding the title prior to my Grandmommy and my Great Aunt Char, and I had been working at the radio station and was going through an interviewing phase of my life.

I took my tape recorder up when we visited that summer and asked her questions about as far back as she could remember. She shared stories of ancestors coming over on the boat from "the old country," which, when I asked about, she referred to as Prussia. She told me as much as she could remember about her parents and extended family. Her mother was a laundress and had worked for a wealthy family in Chicago and had ironed linens for the Astors when they visited. I was glad to be able to gather her stories and piece together some information on names I had heard over the years. Nana died in 1997, and I was so glad I had recorded those memories.

However, it didn't help that my boxes were nicely labeled boxes when, two years later, the basement flooded and went undetected until all the possessions were beyond salvageable. Digitalization wasn't common practice (I don't even know if it existed beyond libraries) and that

tape was my only copy. Lost again were all of my mementos—this time my college photo albums and year-
books, the lovely pillow my sorority big sister made me
that I loved and put away so it wouldn't get ruined. The
only things that I had left were one portfolio of black-
and-white photos I had taken during college that was
upstairs in the office and one shoebox of things that was
on the table next to my bed. All gone, yet again, but the
thing that I was most upset about was that tape with my
Nana's interview because not only was there no copy,
but I had not transcribed it, thinking I'd get around to
it someday. All of those stories, her history in her own
words, lost.

In addition to the lesson about labeling the boxes, I
had now learned not to put treasures in the basement,
and from then on kept them upstairs in the office. The
third time it was scrapbooks and again boxes of photos
and keepsakes. The scrapbooks were ones I had put together from the kids' childhoods. I made sure to save
it all so that they would have everything: every report
card, birthday card, photos with Santa, all the things
from their childhood since I had lost those from mine.
I had a box of photos and keepsakes for every year, labeled of course.

Additionally I had one box of mementos that had
managed to survive the former catastrophes: college
transcripts, my high school diploma, the high school
graduation letter from my uncle, the letter that I would
have loved to share with my cousins. It had photos from
my 20s and 30s. There were keepsakes I received of my

grandmothers after they passed away. One of these was the war ration book Grandmommy had when my Poppa was away in WWII and she was a young mother who used the stamps to purchase things such as sugar and milk, some stamps still there, never used. It had her name and the date in someone's fountain pen script. The box also had the photos that my grandmother carried in her wallet and her social security card.

I lost all of it the third time after my divorce. When I went to collect my things, I was told they were not there. When I tried pursuing it, I was unsuccessful and unfortunately, my ex-husband liked to have backyard bonfires. Thankfully, my kids had a few keepsakes in their bedrooms that we now have, but the majority was lost.

I hope you can learn from my mistakes and that as you reflect and connect with others that you also save and store. Any of the documents, the sentiments shared—emails, letters, photos—save them digitally along with a backup so that you have them not only for you and the person you share with to look back on, but for historical purposes for families and friends to look back on. Being able to remember the essence of someone in words is one thing, but to actually see them in a photo or video or hear their voice or see their handwriting, it just means so much more. I continue to be sentimental with keepsakes, probably to the point of attachment, but because I have lost them not once, but three times; I think that's understandable. Not having them can leave you feeling like you are missing the "proof" of that time, that you really were there: you were a part of that team, or that play or family reunion. It requires you to rely on memories to feel that connection and sense of belonging in that moment or experience.

FRIENDLY INCLUSION

Sometimes, you encounter someone who just makes you feel welcome and like you belong. My friend Brett was like that. I met him because his mother worked with my dad and he was on the swim and tennis team in the summers with me. He was another one who always had a way of making everything feel like an adventure was afoot and would create games and scenarios in the swim pool and was a leader without being bossy or aggressive. People just naturally wanted to join in with whatever game or adventure he was cooking up.

I especially appreciated this because I felt like an outsider with the friend groups during the summer. Actually, one girl, in the honest way only kids can be to each other, did not forget to remind me that "you know you're not a real club member, don't you?" and that was something that stuck. And I felt like that, not 100% part of the group. Except when we were doing something that included Brett because he made everyone feel equally important, like the games wouldn't be the same without them.

Brett made me feel like it wasn't stupid to try out yet again for cheerleading in high school. I had tried out in eighth grade and didn't make it. After tryouts you would have to wait a few hours as they tallied up the scores, and then they would post the list of who made it on the doors of the side entrance of the middle school. I remember standing on my toes to look as the swarms of girls flocked to the list. My name was not there, and I tried to put on a brave face while others were jumping around in celebration. One of the gym teachers who had served as a judge pulled me aside. She told me I missed making it by one point, and she decided to tell me because she wanted me to know that I was so close. She didn't want me to give up, but try again next year.

In ninth grade, I tried again. This time, they posted the list on the front glass doors of the high school and, again, my name was not on the list. One person ended up leaving the district at the end of the year, which left a spot open. We were notified they would be letting the alternate know, and I was hopeful that it was me, but I was not notified that I was the alternate. This time, one of the judges found me and asked to talk to me. She said she wanted me to try again next year, because I was so close. And I said, "Oh, I know, I was next in line, right, missed it by a point or two?" And she said, "No, you were the alternate." She explained that the uniform had already been ordered for the original girl, so they needed someone who would fit in the uniform, which was a size Small. I was not a size Small. I was heartbroken and shared the news with Brett.

I decided the next year that I would try one more time. If it didn't work out, that was it. I'd be done. I practiced with a couple of older girls on the Varsity squad who had been on the dance squad with me and was hopeful once more. Once again, that awful anticipation as they went to post the list. As I pushed my way through the group crowding around the paper, I saw my name! I couldn't believe it. I checked twice and then went and actually touched the paper, tracing my name to make sure. I turned around and saw Brett, who was returning from a tennis tournament. He looked at me and I nodded, and he ran up to me and gave me the biggest hug and spun me around!

He went away to college, and we lost touch for a few years. But junior year, he went to my college for a year. It was amazing to reconnect with him and introduce him to my college friends. In true Brett fashion, he ended up doing the same thing he did in grade school, middle school and high school. He befriended and brought everyone around him together. He made everyone feel like they belonged, and he was happy to be with them. He just has that quality.

~

HOMETOWNS

I grew up in a small town where everyone knew everyone and everyone's business. As a young child, this was comforting but as I grew, not so much. You were bound to encounter a friend's parent or your teachers or Brownie leaders. Wherever you went, you'd run into someone. Once I had reached the age of probably 10, I had lost patience for running errands with my parents, with my mom especially because she always ran into someone she knew. Inevitably, they would strike up a conversation and in addition to wanting to be anywhere else, I didn't know what the correct protocol was. Should I try to look like I wasn't paying attention to be overhearing things that I shouldn't be, or should I nod in acknowledgement signaling that I was listening and not zoning out and being rude? I certainly didn't want them asking me any questions. Sometimes, I took to waiting in the car when she was running into a store, or the post office for "just one thing," but that was not always a winning situation either, with sticky car seats and 90+ degree weather with the sun beating in through the windshield or in the dead of winter with the car turned off so there was no heat and you were breathing and fogging up the windows.

Later, this changed to not wanting to be seen with a boy, or with friends that parents didn't exactly approve of, or doing something someone might tattle on you about. It was really annoying to feel like you could not go anywhere without risking running into someone, someone with a big mouth, and there seemed to be more big mouths than little mouths in my town. We lived in dread of the morning news reports on the local radio when my brother was in high school, not knowing if he and his friends had t.p.'d a house and we'd hear about it on the news. I hated that there was no anonymity, and I couldn't wait to grow up and leave and move to a more urban area. I had big dreams of New York or California, anywhere but Jacksonville, surrounded by corn and soybean fields, FFA jackets a blanket of blue in the halls at school.

I did eventually move away. Not to New York, (I did, however briefly, call California home) but another state in the Midwest. After my parents retired, they moved away too, closer to me so they could be near the grand-kids, and then my brothers followed. We are all near each other once again. Since my parents moved away from our hometown, there hasn't been much of a reason to return. I hadn't been back in over a decade. I've been back the past couple years with my kids. I took them by the houses where I grew up and around town pointing out where some of my childhood milestones and memo-ries were—schools, tennis courts, first job, etc.

The most recent trip was made to honor and celebrate a family friend who had gone before her time. During the eulogies, I was overcome by a couple of realizations. The first one being a surprise that she had done so much, seen so much, and how well defined she was. People had a sense of who she was, and almost everyone's percep-tions matched—she loved her dogs, she spoke her mind, you always knew where you stood with her, her family was everything to her. She was a teacher, both by pro-fession and just by her nature, often showing off her fish pond and gardens to neighbors, classes of students, and other passersby. I realized not only what a magnificent person she was, how many lives she had touched, how many students she taught, how many adventures she'd had with different groups and the activities and clubs she was in, and they were all there to honor her, to reflect and share what she meant to them. I also realized how living in a small community is a gift itself.

It's in the support you receive, the genuine care and concern, the people who show up for you, in good times, but especially in the bad. It's in the traditions of certain places people go to for generations. I realized how lucky I was to grow up in such a place; that it is a foundation for how I see the world. A place where I felt safe, we didn't always lock our door, and our friends all knew where the key was "hidden." On this trip, I was able to see and catch up with my first and second grade teachers, families we had vacationed with, and with whom I spent many nights sleeping over at their home. I was able to see my first hairstylist, who is still cutting hair. And these people remembered me after 40+ years. It was humbling and heartwarming. That's a small town. That's a close community. That's belonging.

REFLECT AND CONNECT

In looking back at your childhood, can you recall times and people that were significant to your sense of community and belonging?

- Who included you at a time when you were feeling like an outsider or like you didn't fit in? What did they do that made you feel included?
- Do you have some prized possessions that remind you of a time you were part of a team or group?

- Can you think of a few photos or letters or pieces of memorabilia you'd like to digitize so you don't lose them?
- What is a practice or ritual that was comforting or made you feel like you belonged?
- Are there some traditions or celebrations of your hometown that made you feel a sense of community? Are there any that you still return there to participate in?
- Do you feel differently about your hometown now as an adult? Who are some of the people you now appreciate even more?

Reach out and share the memories that surfaced. Find old friends on social media, share a photo from that time with them. Share your gratitude for the memories they were part of or how they made you feel connected.

"Instead of drifting along like a leaf in a river, understand who you are and how you come across to people and what kind of an impact you have on the people around you and the community around you and the world, so that when you go out, you can feel you have made a positive difference."
—Jane Fonda[32]

---

[32] Devaney, Susan. "10 of Jane Fonda's Best Quotes on Love, Life & Activism." British Vogue, 16 Sept. 2020 https://www.vogue.co.uk/arts-and-lifestyle/gallery/jane-fonda-quotes#:~:text=On%20living%20your%20best%20life,have%20made%20a%20positive%20difference.%E2%80%9D

————— CHAPTER 14 —————

GRATEFUL FOR TRADITIONS AND CREATING LEGACY

Traditions can help us connect with our family and friends and contribute to legacy, influencing and linking us to future generations, whether those are traditions we're invited to be a part of or those we initiate ourselves. Some that I've experienced or borrowed I'd like to share here, as I'm grateful for the way being a part of them has connected me to others and brought about a sense of fulfillment and joy.

> "When you learn about the teaching and the practice of another tradition, you always have a chance to understand your own teaching and practice."
> —*Thich Nhat Hanh*[33]

BIRTHDAY LETTERS

When I was pregnant, I read a magazine article written by a daughter. Her father had written her a letter on

---

[33] Thich Nhat Hanh. "Extended Interview." *Religion & Ethics Newsweekly*, PBS, 19 Sept. 2003, https://www.pbs.org/wnet/religionandethics/2003/09/19/september-19-2003-extended-interview-thich-nhat-hanh/2758/. Accessed 11 Dec. 2024.

her birthday every year from age 1 to 21. After her father passed away, she was presented with the bundle of letters she didn't know existed. And it was such a gift to her, a beautiful connection to him and a side to him she had never known, thoughts he had through her growing up years, feelings he had never expressed. It gave her a whole new appreciation for him, for what he noticed, for how he felt about her, and it brought another level of closeness to her memories and enhanced the legacy he left for her.

That tradition moved me, and I have done the same. Each year, on or during the week of their birthday, I have written my son and daughter birthday letters. Usually, when we take the card display down, I take back the birthday card I gave them and tuck the letter inside that, so they get the double whammy- both the letter and the card that usually reflects whatever they were interested in at the time (Wiggles, Madeline, etc.) In those letters I share with them what they were up to at the current age, telling them my hopes, fears, and wishes for them. And while I can't say that during the young hectic years when I was working and chasing kids and going to grad school that I have a letter for every single year, I do have one for most of them and look forward to giving them to my kids soon, on their 21st birthdays, and I sure hope they sit down and read them (Max!) and know how much I have loved being their mom.

~

THE TRADITION OF THE MOTHER & DAUGHTER CHRISTMAS TEA

As a teenager, I babysat for a family I adore, a family with a daughter and two sons. They had one of the sweetest holiday traditions that I was lucky enough to be part of as it is one of my many fond annual holiday memories from my hometown. Beginning in 1979, Addie and Laura hosted an annual Mother & Daughter Christmas Tea where friends could socialize and celebrate the season. It provided an atmosphere of mother/daughter bonding and gave all the girls the opportunity to wear their fancy Christmas dresses for something other than pictures and school programs. It became a tradition that the mothers and daughters looked forward to each year, and it chronicled, through a scrapbook on display each year and a guest book the girls would sign, the girls' growth from toddlers to young ladies. I was invited to early teas as a guest with my mother and, when I was older, I helped serve at the tea.

When I became a mother of a daughter myself, I wanted to continue this beautiful tradition for our family and create some mother/daughter memories of our own. Addie was gracious and shared some old photos of the original tea days and recipes that I replicated that became anticipated treats by the girls each year. It was a way to honor and remember Addie & Laura's traditions and welcome the holiday season warmly and in good company. I am thankful for those memories of the teas that my daughter and I hosted and hope someday, my daughter will continue the tradition.

RESOURCES FOR CREATING LEGACY

In closing, I'd like to share some resources that I've been grateful for as they have inspired me, helped me connect with others, elicited memories, and facilitated sharing stories and grateful moments.

Storyworth has simplified capturing your "story of a lifetime" in a unique and approachable way. They send an email each week to the recipient, asking questions about their lives, which can be tailored to the things the author wants to share or any co-subscribers want to discover. At the end of the 52 weeks, they compile and send a lovely quality hard-cover book, including all of the responses and any photos uploaded, creating the story of their life. I bought this for both of my parents. We completed my dad's, and my mom is still working on hers. Even if someone is unable to type or has memory issues, this is still something you can do with and for them. Each time I visited my dad that year, I would pull up the weekly question and ask him, and then I would type and submit his responses. I learned a lot of stories I hadn't heard before, and it allowed him to reminisce. The book that arrived will be enjoyed by our family for years to come.

Chronicle Books makes an amazing series called Letters to My...(father, mother, etc.) for specific people in your life. The books include a dozen or so folded letters with a prompt at the top to respond to. You can tear out the letters or keep them in the book for a nicely packaged presentation. A friend introduced me to these letter books one year by giving me one for my daughter. Last year, I sought out the dad version after we learned about his illness. I was able to complete the book of letters before he progressed too far in his illness to not be able to remember what I wrote about. My mom read the letters to him, so she was able to share in the memories, too. I felt a sense of closure at being able to tell him about some of the special moments we had and what I remember about them, sharing my gratitude for those moments. The prompts in the book are universal and easy to respond to. Each is on a one-page letter that you then fold, seal, and date. It's a quick and meaningful way to share.

Kat Short and her offerings that are continually evolving has been a source of creative inspiration for storytelling. She introduced and shepherded her followers through writing a chap book—a small, yet manageable way to self-publish a meaningful piece of writing. The one I was inspired to write was one for my kids on what it means to be in our family—some of the traditions and funny sayings, songs, foods, that are part of our story, so that as they go out into the world, when they need a reminder of what home is, what it means to be in our family, they are reminded of their foundation.

Kat also shared another take on the birthday letters. Each year on her birthday, she writes herself a letter about what is going on in her life and what she is wishing for in the coming year. I have started doing this too, reflecting on what I'm grateful for the past year, recounting some of the highlights. I also include what I'm looking forward to or hoping for. She is currently sharing newsletters in Substack, *The Quintessence*. Check out her website, www.katshort.com, for her latest offerings. Through her beautiful prose, she touches the soul in a delicate and profound way, inspiring us to examine and express what matters most.

Grand Exit podcast shares about legacy and living. The hosts get real and talk about life, death, and legacy and urge you to really explore how you want to be remembered, particularly poignant as one of the hosts, Tamatha, is living with metastatic cancer. She shares the lessons she's learned, how she wants to be remembered, and the legacy she is leaving.

This resonates with me around the theme of gratitude in a few ways. First, the topics they discuss foster communication and important conversations with those in our lives. When we have those discussions with our loved ones, they learn about us, about what is important to us, and why they are important to us. They encourage us to think about the legacy we are leaving and to write our own eulogies so that we can reflect on how we are living our lives, what we are grateful for, how we want to be remembered. Doing this can be confronting in identifying where we are not meeting our own goals, hopes, and dreams. This enables us to course-correct and take action— another thing to be thankful for. Grand Exit put together a 40 *Living Questions* guide that is fabulous for sparking conversations around living, remembering, and legacy.

You can listen to Grand Exit with Tamatha and Chelsea and find out about their latest offerings, wherever you get your podcasts.

The Traveling Table for connection inspiration.

The Traveling Table Dinner Series (https://www.andhuman.space/thetravelingtable) is hosted by Lia James who magically creates experiences where people meet over a meal, prepared by local food vendors from underserved communities that she partners with, on a table she handcrafted herself(!) to share meaningful conversations and connect.

Not only is it a beautiful concept and insightful experience for those participating, but the meals shared at the Traveling Table are recorded so viewers can witness, identify and connect with those at the table. She brings together a group of people with varying perspectives to discover their similarities, while celebrating their differences and learning from each other. How much more thankful would we be for each other if only we could sit down and share a meal together, human to human?

Childhood songs that I listened to as I wrote helped to bring back the memories, the feelings and sense of those days long ago. I realized how grateful I am for music and how it enhances our experiences, how it's tied to almost every milestone memory I have. Here is the song list of my childhood, my own extended "mix tape." If you are of my gen (X), it may bring back some memories for you too.

SIDE A- ELEMENTARY MY DEAR

Joy to the World - Three Dog Night
Copacabana - Barry Manilow
Bad, Bad, Leroy Brown - Jim Croce
Lyin' Eyes - Eagles
Dancing Queen- Abba
Fire and Rain - James Taylor
Stayin' Alive - Bee Gees
Bridge Over Troubled Water - Simon & Garfunkel
We Are The Champions - Queen
Y.M.C.A - Village People
Annie's Song - John Denver
I Am Woman - Helen Reddy
Rock with You - Michael Jackson
Let's Groove - Earth, Wind & Fire
I Think I Love You - Partridge Family
Dust In The Wind - Kansas
The Boxer - Simon and Garfunkel
Peace Train- Cat Stevens
You Light Up My Life - Debby Boone
You're So Vain - Carly Simon
Another Brick in the Wall - Pink Floyd

SIDE B-HIGH SCHOOL DAYS

The Boys of Summer -Don Henley
Take On Me - A-Ha
Pretty In Pink- Psychedelic Furs
Melt With You - Modern English
Mad World - Tears for Fears
Total Eclipse of the Heart - Bonnie Tyler

Tainted Love - Soft Cell
If You Leave - OMD
Don't You (Forget About Me) Simple Minds
Walk Like an Egyptian - Bangles
Walk on the Wild Side - Lou Reed
Come On Eileen - Dexys Midnight Runners
Let's Dance - David Bowie

Cruel Summer - Bananarama

CONNECT

The last few prompts I'll leave you with are:

- What are some traditions you do with your family that you hope your family will continue?
- A challenge to make your own childhood mix/ playlist that you share with your kids or friends and family.
- Try a twist on the birthday letter tradition by making it a collaboration. Write a letter on special days or milestones and include a photo from a prior year that describes what you remember from that moment. Then ask others to contribute. They can write and add what they remember, making it a collective remembrance that you share with the recipient.

REFLECT

Since I began writing this book, more friends and loved ones have lost family members. We found out last week that one of the basketball players who came to visit my dad last summer died. We were so saddened to learn this and never could have guessed that my dad with his health issues would have outlived him. It reinforces how short our time is and that tomorrow isn't promised.

As we age, we understand this more urgently. My friends and I are in what they call the sandwich generation, still taking care of our children, but also needing to care for parents. Please don't leave things unsaid. Share your gratitude while you can. We all could use a little care and gratitude. Just reach out and say thank you to someone today. Waiting doesn't do any good. Keeping it to yourself robs you of the joy of reflection and appreciation. It also robs the recipient of not knowing how much they matter to you.

This is my thank you, me sharing my gratitude to a small subset of people who have touched my life, changed me, and helped me become who I am. I am so thankful for your influence and role in my life. I'm grateful for the experience of reflecting, for the days when I could immerse myself in memories, and boost my spirit with songs from childhood, and even for those many days when I struggled to recall something; oh, it's just on the tip of my tongue...I'm thankful for the experience of finally writing a book. I'm so grateful to you for reading it.

ACKNOWLEDGEMENTS

I'm immensely grateful for all of the help along the way; it's been a long road, and there have been several people who helped me see this through and would not let me quit.

Thank you to the Hope Books author cohort for answering questions, Brian Dixon, who leads us and teaches us each and every week, and to the Hope Media team for supporting and keeping us on task. I'd like to especially thank my editor, Abby McDonald, for her guidance (and patience).

To my early readers for your time, attention to detail, and willingness to point out where there were improvements to be made: Danielle Alsky, Charlotte Burchill, Kristina Clarke, Paula Payton Gurrie, and Stephanie Melin.

Max Burchill for the back cover photo.

Gayathri Kamath for writing advice, software suggestions, and fountain pen knowledge.

"Book Club" members who showered me with enthusiasm about writing this book: Kristina Clarke, Justina Lampman, Jayme Lanker, Michelle Lanzi, Donna Paulson, and Julie Wigley.

Release The Bees Writing group for the support and laughs through the winding writing path we've been on together for over two decades (has it really been that long?!?): Gina Boldman, Joanna Brod, Paula Payton Gurrie, Melinda Krasner, Harry Levine, Pam Patterson, Wendy Sherrill, Karen Simpson, Debbie Taylor, Jeff Wolf. Also, we cannot forget our early member, Tris Jahanian. You all are an inspiration, and I've always loved the variety of writing across our group and how I continue to learn from you.

To my small group "girls": Beth Desormeaux, Karen Latta, and Debbie Wood for their support– "We are small, but we are mighty!"

To my sister-in-law, the other Jennifer Gay, for her encouragement and for enhancing our family, I can't imagine us without you.

Ginger for keeping my feet warm on many winter weekend writing mornings.

And most of all, my favorite son, Max, and my favorite daughter, Charlotte, who believed I had a story to share.